Department of Health

Independent Health Care

National Minimum Standards Regulations

LEARNING RESOURCES
CENTRE
Havering College
of Further and Higher Education

London: TSO

Published by TSO (The Stationery Office) and available from:

Online
www.tso.co.uk/bookshop

Mail, Telephone, fax & E-mail
TSO
PO Box 29, Norwich NR3 1GN
Telephone orders/General enquiries 0870 600 5522
Fax orders 0870 600 5533
E-mail: book.orders@tso.co.uk
Textphone 0870 240 3701

TSO Shops
123 Kingsway, London WC2B 6PQ
020 7242 6393 Fax 020 7242 6394
68–69 Bull Street, Birmingham B4 6AD
0121 236 9696 Fax 0121 236 9699
9–21 Princess Street, Manchester M60 8AS
0161 834 7201 Fax 0161 833 0634
16 Arthur Street, Belfast BT1 4GD
028 9023 8451 Fax 028 9023 5401
18–19 High Street, Cardiff CF10 1PT
029 2039 5548 Fax 029 2038 4347
71 Lothian Road, Edinburgh EH3 9AZ
0870 606 5566 Fax 0870 606 5588

TSO Accredited Agents
(see Yellow Pages)

and through good booksellers

Published for the Department of Health under licence from the Controller of Her Majesty's Stationery
Office.

First published 2002
Third impression 2004

ISBN 0 11 322572 5

Web Access

This document is available on the DoH internet web site at:
www.doh.gov.uk/ncsc

National Minimum Standards and Regulations for Independent Health Care

A statement of national minimum standards published by the Secretary of State for Health under section 23(1) of the Care Standards Act 2000.

February 2002

National Minimum Standards for Independent Health Care

Note

This document contains a statement of national minimum standards published by the Secretary of State under section 23(1) of the Care Standards Act 2000. The statement is applicable to independent hospitals, independent clinics and independent medical agencies (as defined by section 2 of that Act).

The statement is accompanied, for explanatory purposes only, by an introduction to the statement as a whole, and a further introduction to each group of standards.

Each individual standard is numbered and consists of the numbered heading and numbered paragraphs. Each standard is, for explanatory purposes only, preceded by a title and an indication of the intended outcome in relation to that standard.

Department of Health

Contents

Introduction

Aims

This document sets out regulations and national minimum standards for independent health care, which the new National Care Standards Commission (NCSC) will use to determine whether providers of independent health care have in place appropriate safeguards and quality assurance arrangements for their patients.

The regulations and standards will apply to independent health care establishments for which registration is currently required under the Registered Homes Act 1984, and to independent health care providers who will be newly regulated by the NCSC from April 2002 (ie exclusively private doctors, hyperbaric oxygen chambers and establishments where treatment is provided using intense light sources). A list of the types of independent health care providers to be regulated is at Appendix A.

Regulatory Context

The regulations and standards are published by the Secretary of State for Health in accordance with section 23 of the Care Standards Act 2000 (CSA). They will apply from 1 April 2002.

The CSA sets out a broad range of regulation-making powers covering, amongst other matters, the management, staff, premises and conduct of social and health care establishments and agencies. Section 23 gives powers to the Secretary of State to publish statements of national minimum standards that the NCSC must take into account when making its decisions. These standards will form the basis for judgements made by the NCSC about registration and the imposition of conditions for registration, variation of any conditions and enforcement of compliance with the CSA and associated regulations, including proceedings for cancellation of registration or prosecution. The NCSC will therefore consider the degree to which a regulated service complies with the standards when determining whether or not a service should be registered or have its registration cancelled, or whether to take any action for breach of regulations.

Project Method

The regulations and standards in this document have been produced by taking account of a wide range of influences. These include the Health Select Committee's *Fifth Report on the Regulation of Private and Other Independent Healthcare* (1999); the quality assurance schemes that some providers currently apply to their services; the format and some of the content of the regulations and standards against which the NCSC will regulate care homes; and the standards that apply in the NHS, including the relevant National Service Frameworks and the Controls Assurance Standards.

The preliminary views of patients groups, providers, regulators, insurers and bodies representing the professions who provide services in the establishments and agencies to be regulated, including points raised leading up to, during and after the passage of the CSA, have also been taken into account in producing the regulations and national minimum standards.

The regulations and standards were also subject to a full public consultation exercise between July and October 2001. A report on the consultation is available on the Department of Health's website at www.doh.gov.uk/ncsc

Structure and Approach

The regulations and national minimum standards for independent health care focus on ensuring that patients receive treatment and services in independent health care establishments, or provided by independent medical agencies, that are safe and quality-assured.

The national minimum standards consist of core standards that apply to all independent health care providers regulated by the NCSC, supplemented by service-specific standards that apply to the relevant individual areas of health care services to be regulated. The Private and Voluntary Health Care Regulations follow this core and service-specific format.

Each standard is preceded by a statement of the intended outcome for patients. In order to help to distinguish and identify the standards they are numbered and have prefixes as follows: C for core, A for acute hospitals, M for mental health, H for hospices, MC for maternity hospitals, TP for termination of pregnancy, P for prescribed techniques/technology and PD for private doctors.

Whilst the standards are qualitative – they provide a tool for judging if patients are receiving safe and quality-assured treatment and services – they are also measurable. Regulators will look for evidence that the requirements are being met through:

● discussions with patients, staff and managers and others;

● observation of arrangements in the establishment;

● scrutiny of written policies, procedures and records.

The involvement of lay assessors in the inspection process will help to ensure a focus on the outcomes for patients.

The standards have been drafted on the basis that it is important that they do not conflict with, or are not inconsistent with, other standards or requirements, not only within independent health care but also across the other areas that the NCSC will regulate. It is also important that the standards for independent health care are capable of standing alone as a clear expression of what is required of service providers in the sector.

Key Values

The regulations and national minimum standards for independent health care are based on certain fundamental principles. In applying these regulations and standards, regulators will look for evidence that the policies and day-to-day operation of independent health care establishments and agencies reflect the following:

- patient-centred services – as the stated outcomes of the standards indicate, they are geared towards ensuring that independent health care providers put patient safety and quality assurance at the centre of what they do;

- patient information – linked to this, the standards aim to ensure that patients and prospective patients have clear and accurate information about independent health care providers, and that providers listen to, and publish, feedback from patients;

- accountability – the registered person must take the appropriate steps to fulfil his/her responsibility for ensuring that the regulations and standards are met, so that patients receive treatment and services that are safe and quality-assured;

- safety and quality assurance – the common aim of the standards, from human resources procedures to risk management arrangements to surgical and pathology arrangements to procedures for laser treatment, is to address how safety and quality assurance can be best achieved;

- consistency – the standards are based on the key principle that they need to be compatible with standards in the NHS.

Context and Purpose

These regulations and standards have been prepared in response to extensive consultation and aim to be realistic, proportionate, fair and transparent. They are minimum provisions below which no provider is expected to operate, and are designed to ensure that patients are protected and receive quality-assured treatment.

Contact Point

National minimum standards are issued by the Secretary of State for Health, but it is the responsibility of the National Care Standards Commission to apply them through regulation to the circumstances of individual establishments, agencies and institutions. The Commission will therefore advise on the standards' application in particular circumstances. Other queries – for example about the policies behind the standards – can be addressed to the Department of Health at this e-mail address: dhmail@doh.gsi.gov.uk.

Core Standards

Core Standards

1

Information Provision

Introduction to Standard C1

Information provision relates to the information that the regulated body produces for external consumption. This covers, for instance:

- advertisements and other promotional material aimed at prospective patients;
- information that the NCSC may wish to collect for its own purposes. The NCSC will require information for regulation purposes, but it may also want to gather other information, for example the number of patients who have to be transferred to NHS hospitals from a particular provider.

An information provision policy must ensure that information published by the establishment or agency about its services is accurate. Concern has been expressed about misleading information given by some independent health care providers to patients and prospective patients as to what the treatment on offer will be likely to achieve. We wish to ensure that information/advertisements that regulated bodies provide about their services are accurate and not misleading.

The standards refer to a patients' guide that each provider will be required, through the Private and Voluntary Health Care Regulations, to produce. The regulations will also require each provider to produce a statement of purpose of the establishment or agency, which must be made available for patients.

The regulations also require various types of information to be made available to the NCSC or supplied to it as a matter of course.

See also, in particular, regulations 6 to 8 and 28 to 30, and Schedule 1 of the Private and Voluntary Health Care Regulations.

Information for Patients

> **OUTCOME**
>
> Patients receive clear and accurate information about their treatment and its likely costs.

STANDARD C1

C1.1 **The establishment or agency has available for prospective patients and their families a patients' guide expressed in clear, relevant language and in a format suitable for the patient profile of the establishment or agency with regard to language and translation, patients with sensory disabilities or patients with learning disability.**

C1.2 The patients' guide is reviewed annually to ensure the information in it remains up to date.

C1.3 The patients' guide includes information about how to make comments, suggestions or complaints about the establishment or agency's services.

C1.4 Patients are advised about how to make suggestions and comments about the patients' guide.

C1.5 The registered person ensures that information on the services provided by the establishment or agency is not misleading and information provided to patients and prospective patients and their families is accurate and that any claims made in respect of services are justified.

C1.6 Any advertisements meet the requirements of the Advertising Standards Authority.

C1.7 Any information given to the media respects the confidentiality of the patients, their families, their carers and staff.

2

Quality of Treatment and Care

Introduction to Standards C2 to C7

Patient safety and quality assurance are the cornerstones of the new regulatory system for independent health care. These regulations and standards therefore seek to ensure that treatment and care is patient-centred and that effective monitoring of clinical care takes place. Towards this end, and to help demonstrate the measures they have taken, independent health care providers will be required to have written policies and procedures in place covering various aspects of their activities (see Appendix D). They will also be required to evaluate these policies and procedures to assess their effectiveness.

We expect that the time-scale for evaluation will be set out in the individual written policies. Some policies and procedures will need to be evaluated more often than others (for example, following changes through evidence-based practice or research), but the overall principle is that they must be evaluated/reviewed at least every three years. The evaluation/review can be carried out by the provider itself or by bringing in an external organisation.

In addition to the standards under this quality heading, regulations and standards under the other headings in this consultation document contain measures that contribute towards the overall ethos of patient-centred care and quality, for instance in connection with human resources, complaints management, risk management, information provision and throughout the service-specific standards. Taken together, these can be seen as requiring independent health care providers to have clinical governance arrangements in place.

The regulations require policies and procedures to be in place that ensure that the competence of each patient to give consent to treatment is assessed and that informed consent to treatment is obtained. The standards refer to the need for the patient's *written* consent before treatment that involves significant risks or side effects. Consent is often wrongly equated with a patient's signature on a consent form. A signature on a form is evidence that the patient has given consent, but is not *proof* of valid consent. If a patient is rushed into signing a form, on the basis of too little information, the consent may not be valid, despite the signature. Similarly, if a patient has given valid verbal consent, the fact that they are physically unable to sign the form is no bar to treatment. Patients may, if they wish, withdraw consent after they have signed a form; the signature is evidence of the process of consent-giving, not a binding contract.

The Government wants a strong public voice in health and health care decision-making. The NHS Plan, for instance, makes it clear that patients are the most important people in the health service. It is equally important that patients in the independent health care sector have a say about the quality of the treatment and care being provided and that their views are heard. In line with measures in the NHS, independent health care providers will be required to carry out patient surveys, the outcome of which will be published annually and made available to patients and prospective patients (and supplied to the NCSC) as part of a patients' guide that each provider will be required to produce.

These core standards, and the service-specific standards that supplement them, have been drafted so as to be, where possible, compatible with 'quality' standards in the NHS.

See also, in particular, regulations 15 to 17 of the Private and Voluntary Health Care Regulations.

Patient-centred Care

OUTCOME
The treatment and care provided are patient-centred.

STANDARD C2

C2.1   **The registered person has policies and procedures in place to ensure that the care provided is patient-centred, as follows:**

- **assessment of patients' health needs are carried out in line with procedures to be timely, appropriate and accurate;**

- **patients are informed of the recommended interventions for treatment and/or care;**

- **patients give verbal consent to all intimate examinations, and are offered a chaperone if undergoing such an examination, or are able to bring a relative or friend with them if they wish;**

- **patients, and their relatives if appropriate, are consulted about the planning and delivery of services provided to them, which includes taking into account their preferences and requests;**

- **patients have access to their health records in line with the Data Protection Act 1998;**

- **patients' rights are central to the resuscitation policy;**

- **services are provided in such a way that facilitates access by people of different cultural and ethnic backgrounds and those with physical disabilities, sensory disabilities and learning disabilities;**

- **patients' privacy, dignity and confidentiality are respected at all times;**

- **patients are addressed by their preferred name and title;**

- **patients are treated with courtesy and consideration.**

C2.2   DH guidance (Department of Health Guidance *Reference Guidance to Consent for Examination or Treatment*) on consent to treatment, including consent by children and the concept of 'Gillick Competencies', is followed.

C2.3   Clinical procedures are explained to patients so that they understand the implications of the treatment and any options available to them, allowing them to give valid consent or refusal (including discharging themselves against medical advice), which is documented in the patient's health record.

C2.4   Patients give written consent before receiving treatment where:

- the treatment or procedure is complex, or involves significant risks or side-effects;

- general/regional anaesthetic or sedation is to be used;

- clinical care is not the primary purpose of the procedure;

- there may be significant consequences for the patient's employment, social or personal life;

- the treatment is part of a project or programme of research.

C2.5   Completed forms are kept with the patient's notes. Any changes to a form, made after the form has been signed by the patient, are initialled and dated by both patient and health care professional.

C2.6   There is a written policy and procedure to follow when the patient does not have the capacity to give valid consent to treatment.

C2.7   There is a written policy and procedure on how to respond to advance directives (living wills).

C2.8   There are facilities for patients to have confidential discussions with health care professionals that ensure privacy.

C2.9   Staff wear identification badges showing name and position held.

C2.10   Patients who choose not to discuss health related matters with members of the opposite sex receive consultations with health care professionals of the same sex where possible.

C2.11   There are written policies on the prevention of harassment and bullying of patients by staff and or other patients, inline with the UKCC guidance: '*Practitioner/client relationships and the prevention of abuse.*'

Management of Patient Conditions

OUTCOME

Treatment provided to patients is in line with the relevant clinical guidelines.

STANDARD C3

C3.1 **The management of specific conditions takes account of evaluations by the National Institute for Clinical Excellence (NICE) in relation to effective clinical practice and patient safety and specific clinical guidelines from the relevant medical Royal Colleges, healthcare professional institutions and the NHS National Service Frameworks.**

C3.2 Training for health care professionals is provided in meeting the needs of patients with physical disability, sensory disability and/or learning disabilities, appropriate to the patient profile for the establishment.

Monitoring Quality

OUTCOME

Patients are assured that monitoring of the quality of treatment and care takes place.

STANDARD C4

C4.1 **The written policy and procedures for clinical treatment and care include arrangements for monitoring the quality of care provided including:**
- **clinical audit (informed by trends, for instance, in litigation, complaints, clinical outcomes and risk management);**
- **the performance indicators to be used by the establishment and how these are to be reported on;**
- **the outcomes of clinical and nursing audits;**
- **the use of comparative information on clinical outcomes;**
- **evaluation against research findings and evidence based practice;**
- **participation in national confidential enquiries (such as the National Confidential Enquiry into Peri-Operative Deaths);**
- **effective information and clinical record systems;**
- **the identification and recording of the respective and common responsibilities of team members, for example in a job description or role profile;**
- **procedures for identifying and learning from adverse health events and near misses;**
- **a complaints procedure.**

Care of the Dying

OUTCOME

The dying and death of patients is handled appropriately and sensitively.

STANDARD C5

C5.1 **Care and comfort are given to patients who are dying, their death is handled with dignity and propriety, and their emotional, psychological and spiritual needs, rites and functions observed.**

C5.2 Clinical staffing levels are such to allow attention to the physical care needs of the patient and to provide pain relief and symptom control as required.

C5.3 The patient's wishes concerning terminal care and arrangements after death are discussed, if the patient wishes, and documented in the care plan.

C5.4 The patient's family and friends are involved (if that is what the patient wants) in planning for and dealing with terminal illness and death.

C5.5 The privacy and dignity of the patient who is dying are maintained at all times.

C5.6 In situations where the patient death is anticipated, palliative care, practical assistance and advice, and bereavement/support counselling are provided by trained professionals/specialist agencies trained volunteers.

C5.7 The body of a patient who has died is handled with dignity and time allowed for family and friends to view the body in privacy.

Patients' Views

OUTCOME

Patients' views are obtained by the establishment and used to inform the provision of treatment and care and prospective patients.

STANDARD C6

C6.1 **A patient survey is carried out annually, as a minimum, to seek the views of patients on the quality of the treatment and care provided.**

C6.2 The content of the patient survey reflects the content of the NHS patients' survey.

C6.3 The results of the patient surveys are collated annually into a report that is available on request to patients, prospective patients and their families, and is provided to the National Care Standards Commission.

C6.4   The outcome of the surveys are made available to staff and used by the regulated body to contribute to its assessment of whether it is meeting its aims, objectives and statement of purpose.

Policies and Procedures

OUTCOME

Appropriate policies and procedures are in place to help ensure the quality of treatment and services.

STANDARD C7

C7.1   **All staff read the policies and procedures relevant to their area of work and sign a statement to this effect.**

C7.2   Temporary staff are provided with a summary of the clinical and patient care policies pertinent to their area of work and information on where the full policies and procedures are available for reference.

C7.3   There are written policies and procedures for all operational areas within the establishment and these are placed in an accessible position, available to all staff.

C7.4   There is a central register of policies and procedures that includes the title, issue date, review date and circulation of all policy and procedure documents.

C7.5   All policies and procedures are reviewed at least every three years and the date of review is included within each written policy and procedure.

C7.6   The establishment evaluates practice against the policies and procedures to ensure their effective implementation; the evaluation is carried out at least once every three years.

3

Management and Personnel

Introduction to Standards C8 to C13

Registered Person (standard C8)

The role of every person in an independent health care establishment or agency is important in ensuring the delivery of safe quality care, but ultimately the registered provider must be accountable for meeting the standards required for registration, and the registered manager must be accountable for the delivery of the requisite services to those standards. This is a key feature of the new regulatory system. In this respect it is essential that both are fit persons to 'carry on' or manage the establishment or agency and that each have clearly defined roles of responsibility.

The new regulatory regime will require the person 'carrying on' (registered provider) the establishment to be registered with the NCSC, and where that person is not in charge of the day to day running of the business that a manager (registered manager) is appointed and also registered with the NCSC.

Many independent health care establishments will be owned by a company or charity, which may have a number of different establishments throughout the country. In these circumstances the company or charity will be the registered provider. However, it is important that the NCSC has a contact in the organisation for the purposes of communication, and therefore the company will have to provide the NCSC with the name of the 'responsible individual' who is a director, manager, company secretary, or other officer of the organisation. Where the company owns a number of independent health care establishments it will have to register in respect of each one. The person in charge of the day to day running of each establishment will have to register as the manager of the establishment.

Throughout this document the regulations and standards apply to the registered person, that is both the registered provider and the registered manager, unless indicated otherwise.

See also, in particular, regulations 10 to 14 of the Private and Voluntary Health Care Regulations.

Human Resources (standards C9 to C13)

The skill, competence and attitude of those who provide independent health care services are key elements in determining the quality of health care that patients receive.

We wish to ensure that responsibility is placed on those who carry on or manage independent health care to ensure that the people who provide treatment and care in their establishments, or on their behalf, are appropriately skilled, qualified and competent to do so.

To help achieve this the regulations, underpinned by standards, require providers to have a written human resources policy in place, covering the recruitment, induction and retention of employees and their employment conditions. The regulations also set out other staffing requirements, covering assurance about the qualifications and skills of those who work in independent health care establishments and agencies. This is a good example of how the core and service-specific standards interact: the core standards cover human resources and staffing good practice generally, such as training and continuing professional development, and the service-specific standards supplement these by specifying the skills, qualifications and competencies needed for health care professionals working in the individual services regulated.

Those who work in independent health care establishments and agencies have day to day contact with patients, very often on a one-to-one basis. It is therefore essential that the registered person is aware of the 'fitness' of the workers in order to ensure the safety of the patients. The registered person will be required to show that all workers have had their references checked and, where appropriate, ascertain whether the staff are on the Protection of Vulnerable Adults list or on the list held under the Protection of Children Act 1999, and to make a declaration under the Rehabilitation of Offenders Act (see Schedule 2 of the regulations).

The standards relating to pre-employment checks, for example, that they include in their employment application forms a declaration to be completed by the applicant stating whether or not they have been or are the subject of fitness to practice proceedings by any licensing or regulatory body, mirror those that are required in the NHS.

The regulations and standards recognise that the registered person will have some common areas of responsibility both for employed staff and for those practitioners who are given practising privileges in the regulated establishment.

The regulations and standards also recognise that there are differences in the registered person's relationship with each of the two groups. These differences are indicated by the references in the standards to 'staff' (i.e. all those employed by the regulated body, this includes agency staff) and 'personnel' (i.e. those who work in the regulated establishment/agency, including those with practising privileges).

These human resources standards, and the associated regulations, are appropriate even where the independent health care establishment/agency regulated is a single-handed operation, for example a lone private GP. In those circumstances, the registered provider (the GP) will be held accountable under the Care Standards Act for ensuring that whoever provides services in the establishment (even if only the GP himself) is suitably skilled and competent.

See also, in particular, regulations 18 and 19, and Schedule 2 of the Private and Voluntary Health Care Regulations.

Role and Responsibilities of the Registered Manager

OUTCOME

Patients are assured that the establishment or agency is run by a fit person/ organisation and that there is a clear line of accountability for the delivery of services.

STANDARD C8

C8.1 **The manager can demonstrate that he/she has undertaken periodic training to update their knowledge, skills and competence to manage the establishment.**

C8.2 The job description of the registered manager sets out his/her responsibilities to run the establishment in accordance with the law and the national minimum standards.

C8.3 There are clear lines of accountability within the establishment and these are described in an up-to-date organisational structure document or diagram.

C8.4 The registered manager ensures that all relevant certificates and licences which are legally required are obtained, kept up to date and displayed where required.

Human Resources Policies and Procedures

OUTCOME

Patients receive care from appropriately recruited, trained and qualified staff.

STANDARD C9

C9.1 **There is a written human resources policy and supporting procedures, in line with current employment legislation.**

C9.2 There are pre- and post-employment procedures that:

- define the way in which advertising, selection, recruitment, induction, employment and retention of staff is managed;

- ensure that at the short listing stage, prior to making an unconditional offer of employment, a declaration is obtained from a successful applicant as to whether he/she:

    - is currently the subject of any police investigation and/or prosecution, in the UK or any other country;

    - has ever been convicted of any criminal offence required by law to be disclosed, received a police caution in the UK, or a criminal conviction in any other country;

- is currently the subject of any investigation or proceedings by any body having regulatory functions in relation to health/social care professionals including such a regulatory body in another country;

- has ever been disqualified from the practice of a profession or required to practise it subject to specified limitations following a fitness to practise investigation by a regulatory body, in the UK or another country.

- ensure that all staff are interviewed before employment, and that records of interview and written references are retained;

- ensure that qualifications relevant to the post applied for are verified by validation at the interview;

- ensure that prior to employment, the relevant regulatory/licensing body is asked to confirm whether the applicant is appropriately registered, whether that registration covers the duties to be undertaken and whether there are any restrictions in place or investigations underway;

- ensure that employment references are sought from the two most recent employers prior to making an offer of employment;

- ensure that indemnification is checked and authenticated for health care professionals;

- ensure that documentary proof is maintained of the continuing registration of professional staff with their respective professional regulatory body;

- ensure job specifications, performance review, appraisal and line management arrangements are defined for all staff;

- ensure that the person who is being offered a post has his/her identity confirmed through the presentation of a valid birth certificate, and passport or driving licence;

- ensure that there are arrangements to check that the validity of work permits are verified and that their status is clarified.

C9.3   There are arrangements in place to ensure:
- staff training and continuing professional development;
- all staff, including agency nurses and locum medical staff, undertake an induction programme which includes awareness of the policies and procedures relevant to their area of work and which is signed off when completed and a record kept;
- a training record of all educational and professional development activities is kept for each member of staff;
- the performance of all staff within the organisation is reviewed on an annual basis in a systematic way.

C9.4   There are policies in place:
- that set out the procedures for personnel to follow when gifts are offered from patients and gives guidance on what may and may not be accepted;
- that cover the way in which volunteers, if used, are involved;

- on equality of opportunity, which ensure specific attention is paid at all levels of the organisation to the abolition of any form of less favourable treatment to any member of staff, directly or indirectly, on the grounds of race, gender, sexual orientation, disability, religion or trade union membership;
- on anti-harassment and anti-bullying policies.

Practising Privileges

OUTCOME

Patients receive treatment from appropriately recruited, trained and qualified health care professionals.

STANDARD C10

C10.1 **Where health care professionals are granted practising privileges (ie the grant to a person who is not employed in the establishment of permission to practise in that establishment) there are written policies and procedures on allowing practising privileges.**

C10.2 The following pre and post-employment checks are carried out before a health care professional is granted practising privileges:

- that the practitioner is registered with the appropriate professional regulatory body;
- that the practitioner is trained and is experienced in the type of treatment he/she is given practising privileges to perform;
- that the practitioner declares whether or not he/she:
  - is currently the subject of any police investigation and/or prosecution, in the UK or any other country;
  - has ever been convicted of any criminal offence required by law to be disclosed, received a police caution in the UK, or a criminal conviction in any other country;
  - is currently the subject of any investigation or proceedings by any body having regulatory functions in relation to health/social care professionals including such a regulatory body in another country;
  - has ever been disqualified from the practice of a profession or required to practise it subject to specified limitations following a fitness to practise investigation by a regulatory body, in the UK or another country.
- that the practitioner is interviewed before employment, and that records of interview and written references are retained;
- that qualifications relevant to the post applied for are verified by validation at the interview;

- that the practitioner is appropriately registered, whether that registration covers the duties to be undertaken and whether there are any restrictions in place or investigations underway by the relevant regulatory/licensing body;

- that employment references are sought from the two most recent employers prior to making an offer of employment;

- that indemnification is checked and authenticated;

- that documentary proof is maintained of the continuing registration with the respective professional regulatory body;

- that the procedures for practitioners to follow when gifts are offered from patients, and what may and may not be accepted, are set out;

- that the practitioner who is offered practising privileges has his/her identity confirmed through the presentation of a valid birth certificate, and passport or driving licence;

- that there are arrangements in place for ensuring the validity of work permits are verified and that their status is clarified.

C10.3　There is a written agreement with the practitioner setting out:

- the details of the practising privileges, which includes a stated requirement of the practitioner's availability to attend the establishment within a certain time limit if notified of a problem with a patient;

- that he/she will comply with the organisation's policies and procedures including the complaints procedure, and which requires the practitioner to inform the appropriate person if a complaint is made directly to him/her in the first instance.

- that the practitioner is required to place a copy of all clinical notes relating to care or treatment at the establishment in the patient's health record retained by the establishment.

C10.4　There are arrangements in place for continuing professional development.

C10.5　The practitioner is made aware of the current policies and procedures in the establishment, and a list of the relevant policies and procedures that he or she is expected to be familiar with, is provided.

C10.6　Practising privileges are reviewed for each practitioner every two years, as a minimum and may be reviewed more frequently as a result of concerns about practice or complaints received by the establishment.

Compliance with Professional Codes of Practice

OUTCOME

Patients are treated by health care professionals who comply with their professional codes of practice.

STANDARD C11

C11.1 **All health care professionals are required to abide by published codes of professional practice relevant to their professional role.**

C11.2 There is written information for health care professionals that explicitly states that any breach of such codes is regarded as a disciplinary offence. This may be included in the contract of employment, practising privileges agreement, or staff handbook.

C11.3 All health care professionals take part in the ongoing continuing professional development (CPD) required by their professional body and /or Specialist College, including revalidation requirements of the GMC.

Health Care Workers and Blood Borne Viruses

OUTCOME

Patients and healthcare professionals are not infected by blood borne viruses.

STANDARD C12

C12.1 **All health care workers (including practitioners with practising privileges) comply with Department of Health guidelines on health care workers infected with blood borne virus (hepatitis B, hepatitis C, HIV).**

C12.2 There are written instructions for health care workers and practitioners with practising privileges on the steps required by the establishment in order to ensure their compliance and notification of infection status in line with the guidelines.

C12.3 All health care workers who perform exposure prone procedures are required to provide documentary evidence of their vaccination status with regard to hepatitis B, or to be tested for, and vaccinated against, hepatitis B if there is no evidence of previous vaccination produced.

C12.3 The establishment/agency keeps vaccination records for all health care workers employed and all practitioners with practising privileges.

Child Protection Procedures

OUTCOME

Children receiving treatment are protected effectively from abuse.

STANDARD C13

C13.1 **Where children are treated there are child protection procedures in place, with which all personnel are familiar and are included in the induction programme for new staff.**

C13.2 Procedures for handling allegations of child abuse are consistent with the Department of Health, Department for Education and Employment and Home Office guidance Working Together to Safeguard Children.

C13.3 Procedures for handling allegations of child abuse reflect the procedures of the local Area Child Protection Committee.

C13.4 All staff who care for or treat children are trained to recognise the signs and symptoms of child abuse, and are aware of relevant supporting agencies involved in child protection.

C13.5 All allegations of abuse are examined objectively by a person independent of the registered establishment or agency.

C13.6 A child's wish for privacy and confidentiality is handled in way that is consistent with the need to protect the child.

Complaints Management

Introduction to Standards C14 to C16

The lack of a clear and effective process by which patients are able to complain when dissatisfied with treatment and services is often a weakness in the current system. There have been occasions where dissatisfied patients have been passed from the provider of the health care establishment to the person who undertook the treatment with neither taking responsibility for addressing the patient's concerns. The regulations and standards address this issue by requiring the registered person to have an effective complaints system in place.

Providers will be required to have a written procedure for handling complaints about the services, care and treatment provided in, or on behalf of, their establishments/ agencies and to maintain a register of complaints. They will be required to provide the NCSC with an annual summary of the complaints made and the action taken in response.

In order to be fully effective a complaints procedure must ensure that a patient's complaint has a fair hearing and result in remedial action being taken as appropriate. Patients and prospective patients, their families and carers, need to have information available on the complaints procedure at the outset of their treatment. It is also essential that all those who work in the establishment/agency where the treatment is provided are aware of the complaints procedure, and those involved in its provision or procedural elements are trained in its operation.

The NCSC has a two-fold interest in complaints about independent health care:

- that the registered person has in place a complaints system that complies with the regulations and standards on complaints; and
- that a complaint may indicate non-compliance with a particular regulation or standard.

Where patients are unhappy about how a complaint was handled by the provider or with the outcome he/she can complain to the NCSC. A patient can in fact complain direct to the NCSC, but the NCSC may decide that the complaint should be considered at local level first and return it to the provider for action. Although it will not be appropriate for the NCSC to be involved in seeking compensation for patients, if the complaints process indicates that there has been a regulatory failure by the provider the NCSC will be able to consider the position and take appropriate action, including applying sanctions if necessary.

A NHS patient who is treated under contract in an independent hospital will continue to have access to the NHS complaints procedure. Subject to the terms of the contract, the local resolution stage could be handled by the independent hospital. However, if the NHS patient continues to be unhappy he/she can take the complaint to the next stage of independent review, and if necessary through to the Health Service Ombudsman.

In setting in the standards the time-scales within which a complaint should be processed, consideration was given to those in the NHS complaints procedure, the Local Authority social services procedure and the Independent Healthcare Association complaints procedure. It was decided that it would be more appropriate to align the timeframe with that in the NHS complaints procedure.

It is important that regulated providers make clear to those who work within the establishment or agency that they can raise concerns, through the appropriate channels, about their colleagues' performances with impunity.

See also, in particular, regulation 23 of the Private and Voluntary Health Care Regulations.

Complaints Process

OUTCOME
Patients have access to an effective complaints process.

STANDARD C14

C14.1 **The registered person ensures that there is a written policy and procedures for handling and investigating complaints about all aspects of service, care and treatment provided in, or on behalf of, the establishment/agency and that such a policy includes the stages and time-scales for the process.**

C14.2 All complainants receive a written acknowledgement within two working days of receipt of their complaint (unless a full reply can be sent within five working days).

C14.3 A full response is made within 20 working days of receipt of the complaint, or where the investigation is still in progress, a letter explaining the reason for the delay is sent to the complainant and a full response made within five days of a conclusion being reached.

C14.3 The complaints procedure ensures that the complainant receives written confirmation of the stages of investigation and action taken.

C14.4 The complaints procedure is brought to the attention of all personnel (i.e. all staff, agency staff and practitioners with practising privileges), and they receive training on:

- what constitutes a complaint;
- the procedures for receiving and dealing with a complaint.

C14.5 Those staff involved in the provision and procedural elements of the complaints procedure are trained in its operation.

C14.6 A register of complaints, including information on whether or not the complaint was upheld, the results of investigation, the action taken and the resolution of complaints is maintained.

C14.7 Procedures are in place that enable issues raised in complaints to be learnt from in order to improve practice.

Information for Patients about Complaints

OUTCOME
Patients receive appropriate information about how to make a complaint.

STANDARD C15

C15.1 The complaints procedure or information based upon it is accessible to patients and their family members/carers.

C15.2 Where requested the patient and/or family members or carers are given support in using the complaints procedure.

C15.3 Where care and treatment are provided to children, staff are aware of the difficulties a child faces in expressing concerns or complaints and how the child should be helped to overcome these.

Workers' Concerns

OUTCOME
Personnel are freely able to express concerns about questionable or poor practice.

STANDARD C16

C16.1 Personnel are informed of their duty to express their concerns about questionable or poor practice in accordance with the Public Interest Disclosure Act 1998.

C16.2 Personnel are assured that they will not be penalised at any time for complaining in good faith about poor practice.

C16.3 There is a written policy and procedure for personnel to follow in order to raise their concerns about questionable or poor practice.

5

Premises, Facilities and Equipment

Introduction to Standards C17 to C19

The design and condition of the premises where treatment takes place, and the nature of the facilities and equipment generally, have a considerable impact on the treatment, care and services that patients receive. It is essential, therefore, that the premises, facilities and equipment are suitable to meet the needs of patients safely and effectively.

To this end, the key principles of these standards are that:

- premises are designed and maintained with the safety of patients in mind and ensure that patients' privacy and dignity is protected;
- facilities are designed or procured using relevant skills and expertise so that they effectively deliver treatment and services;
- equipment selected and used within the establishment is wholly appropriate for the treatment provided;
- safe and regular maintenance of equipment takes place, ensuring that equipment is used in accordance with the manufacturer's instructions and is not modified or used for purposes for which it was not designed;
- there is a planned replacement programme for equipment.

See also, in particular, regulations 15 and 25 of the Private and Voluntary Health Care Regulations.

Health Care Premises

OUTCOME

Patients receive treatment in premises that are safe and appropriate for that treatment.

STANDARD C17

C17.1 **There is a preventive maintenance plan that covers all areas of the establishment/agency's buildings.**

C17.2 There is fail-safe emergency lighting in place

C17.3   There are emergency contingency plans for major plant failure, or loss of utilities such as electricity, gas or water supplies.

C17.4   The establishment/agency complies with the requirements of the Health and Safety Executive, the fire authority and the environmental health department.

C17.5   The establishment/agency complies with the requirements of the Disability Discrimination Act, with regard to disabled access to all areas routinely visited by patients.

C17.6   All areas used by patients are well lit, internally and externally.

C17.7   Where patients are required to undress, changing room facilities enable privacy and dignity to be maintained.

C17.8   All in-patients have access to single sex toilet and washing facilities.

C17.9   Safe temperatures are monitored and maintained for hot water supplies and the surfaces of heating appliances (for example radiators) in all areas used by patients.

C17.10 Patient care areas are clean, hygienic and free from noxious smells.

C17.11 Waste is segregated into clinical and non-clinical items and stored in colour-coded bags and containers.

C17.12 Clinical waste is labelled to enable it to be traced back to its point of origin.

C17.13 Clinical waste stored outside the building is kept in locked containers.

C17.14 Records are kept of the thorough examination, by a competent person, of all passenger lifts and the periodic examinations, carried out under a suitable written scheme, by a competent person, of all pressure vessels.

C17.15 There are precautions in place to prevent patients falling from windows.

Condition and Maintenance of Equipment and Supplies

OUTCOME

Patients receive treatment using equipment and supplies that are safe and in good condition.

STANDARD C18

C18.1   Equipment is installed, checked and serviced in compliance with the manufacturer's instructions.

C18.2   Equipment is not modified unless the manufacturer's advice has been sought, and no risk has been identified.

C18.3   All equipment conforms to current health and safety regulations and, where appropriate, there is a planned preventive maintenance and replacement programme.

C18.4   Records are kept of the maintenance and servicing of all equipment.

C18.5   All stock products used in the establishment are used in date order to ensure that at the time of use they are in optimum condition and within expiry dates.

C18.6   Heat sensitive and/or light sensitive items are stored in a controlled environment to keep the items in optimum condition.

Catering Services for Patients

OUTCOME

Patients receive appropriate catering services.

STANDARD C19

C19.1   Food is handled, stored, prepared and delivered in accordance with food safety legislation.

C19.2   All staff who handle food undertake initial training in food hygiene on appointment and annual up-date training thereafter.

C19.3   Each in-patient is offered menu choices for three full meals a day, to include at least one cooked meal option per day.

C19.4   Food is nutritious, balanced and varied and meets any special needs of the patient, including age-related requirements for children and the elderly.

C19.5   Special diets are provided on the advice of professional staff or a dietician, including dietary supplements.

C19.6   Religious or cultural needs are catered for.

C19.7   Food is presented in a manner which is attractive and appealing in terms of texture and flavour.

C19.8   Drinking water is available in all inpatient and outpatient areas.

C19.9   Hot drinks and snacks are available to patients outside of mealtimes.

C19.10 Care staff assist patients to eat, when necessary due to illness or disability.

6

Risk Management Procedures

Introduction to Standards C20 to C26

All health care premises, treatment and services contain elements of risk and hazards that need to be carefully identified, monitored, managed and contained. It is essential, therefore, that independent health care providers have effective safeguards in place to protect patients and those who work within, or have contact with, the premises, treatment and services. We believe that the starting point in achieving this is to require providers to have a comprehensive written risk management policy in place to cover their services and the wide and diverse features found within their premises.

Risk management is a careful examination of what could cause harm to patients, visitors and staff so that the provider can consider whether appropriate precautions have been taken. The risk management policy must include the safeguards that all organisations that employ staff and deliver services are required to have: a health and safety policy, arrangements to manage and learn from emergency or untoward incidents, and formal arrangements for the making and recording of contracts.

The requirement for arrangements to be in place in respect of adverse health events and near misses reflects the recommendations for the NHS contained in the Department of Health reports *An Organisation with a Memory* (2000) and *Building a Safer NHS* (2001).

All providers will continue to have to comply with the requirements of other relevant legislation, including health and safety legislation and EU Directives.

See also, in particular, regulations 9 and 15 (5) of the Private and Voluntary Health Care Regulations.

[See: Department of Health *Resuscitation Policy* (HSC 2000/028)]

Risk Management Policy

OUTCOME

Patients, staff and anyone visiting the registered premises are assured that all risks connected with the establishment, treatment and services are identified, assessed and managed appropriately.

STANDARD C20

C20.1 **The registered person ensures that there is a comprehensive written risk management policy and procedures, which cover:**
- **the identification and assessment of risks throughout the establishment;**
- **the precautions in place control the risks identified;**
- **health and safety;**
- **infection control;**
- **decontamination;**
- **arrangements for the identification, recording, analysing and learning from adverse health events or near misses;**
- **arrangements for responding to emergencies;**
- **protection of vulnerable children and adults, including protection from abuse.**

C20.2 Arrangements are in place for dealing with 'alert letters' in accordance with Department of Health guidance and directions.

C20.3 Arrangements are in place for dealing effectively with 'hazard notices' when these are received.

C20.3 There is a written procedure setting out the responsibilities for informing the National Care Standards Commission and national professional bodies such as the GMC about staff who have been suspended on clinical or professional grounds, or practitioners whose practising privileges have been suspended, restricted or withdrawn on professional or clinical grounds.

C20.4 A named member of staff is identified to receive information from the Medical Devices Agency, and report relevant matters to the Agency (including failure of, and accidents in connection with, medical devices).

C20.5 A named member of staff is identified to receive information from the Medicines Control Agency, and report relevant matters to the Agency.

C20.6 Where in-patient care is provided there is a nurse call system installed throughout the patient care areas of the establishment including all patient bedrooms, toilet and shower/bathrooms.

Health and Safety Measures

OUTCOME
The appropriate health and safety measures are in place.

STANDARD C21

C21.1 Arrangements are in place for obtaining competent health and safety advice.

C21.2 There are written procedures for the classification, storage, collection, transport and disposal of all categories of waste in accordance with health and safety and environmental requirements.

C21.3 Where there is a medical gas line(s), there is a written procedure for any interruption of such a line to be authorised by the registered manager or by a person authorised by the registered manager.

C21.4 The registered manager ensures compliance with relevant legislation including:
- Health and Safety at Work Act 1974;
- Management of Health and Safety at Work Regulations 1999;
- Workplace (Health, Safety and Welfare) Regulations 1992;
- Provision and Use of Work Equipment Regulations 1999;
- Electricity at Work Regulations 1989;
- Health and Safety (First Aid) Regulations 1981;
- Control of Substances Hazardous to Health Regulations (COSHH) 1999;
- Manual Handling Operation Regulations 1992;
- Reporting of Injuries, Diseases and Dangerous Occurrences Regulations (RIDDOR) 1985.

C21.5 All personnel have access to occupational health services.

C21.6 Personnel are provided with protective equipment and clothing to prevent risk of harm or injury to themselves or others.

C21.7 There is a written policy on the moving and handling of patients which sets out the arrangements and equipment in place to minimise the moving and handling of patients manually by staff.

C21.8 All health care staff working directly with patients have annual up-date training in moving and handling them.

C21.9 A record is kept of accidents to patients, visitors and personnel, (for instance, including the number of needle stick injuries by category and location of work of staff).

Medicines Management

> **OUTCOME**
>
> Measures are in place to ensure the safe management and secure handling of medicines.

STANDARD C22

C22.1 Medicines are handled according to the requirements of the Medicines Act 1968 and the Misuse of Drugs Act 1971; and with nursing staff following the UKCC *Guidelines for the Administration of Medicines* (October 2000) and pharmacists their professional Code of Ethics.

C22.2 There is a written medicines policy and procedure, accessible to staff, covering all aspects of medicines systems and medical gases in the establishment/agency, which covers:

- ordering, procurement, receipt, storage, administration and disposal of medicines;

- the action to be taken in case of adverse reactions;

- error reporting, to encourage an open reporting system and a non-blame culture.

C22.3 The medicines required for resuscitation or other medical emergency are accessible and in suitable packaging.

C 22.4 All medicine is administered to a patient with a written prescription or, internal to the hospital, a drug administration chart that has been signed by an authorised prescriber.

C22.5 There is a written policy for the steps to be followed in the exceptional circumstances where a medicine is administered without a written direction, for example, a life-threatening situation.

C22.6 All medicine doses are prepared immediately prior to their administration to patients from the container in which they are dispensed.

C22.7 Medicines prescribed and labelled received against a prescription for a named patient are not used for any other patient.

C22.8 Information is given to patients about the use, benefits and potential harms of medication prescribed.

C22.9 The establishment has access to up-to-date, relevant reference sources, for example the British National Formulary, the Summary of Product Characteristics for every product used and access to evaluated information about medicines.

C22.10 Medicines are used as specified in the Summary of Product Characteristics, unless there is a body of evaluated evidence to support any use outside this licence, in which case patients are informed that the medicine is used outside the Summary of Product Characteristics.

C22.11 When clinical trials take place they are undertaken in accordance with relevant legislation and best practice guidelines and with local research ethics committee approval.

C22.12 When patient group directions are used they comply with Department of Health/Medicines Control Agency guidance.

Ordering and Storage of Medicines

OUTCOME

Medicines, dressings and medical gases are handled in a safe and secure manner.

STANDARD C23

C23.1 **A record is kept of ordering, receipt, supply, administration and disposal of all medicines dressings and medical gases in order to maintain an audit trail.**

C23.2 Lockable storage is provided for:

- controlled drugs in accordance with the Misuse of Drugs (Safe Custody) Regulations 1973;
- medicines for external use;
- medicines for internal use;
- medicines requiring cold storage;
- diagnostic reagents (other than test strips);
- flammable substances.

C23.3 The storage of medical gases should be in accordance with guidance set out in Health Equipment Information No 163,2/87.

C23.4 The keys of all cupboards used for the storage of medicines are held securely, including spare keys.

C23.5 Medicines requiring cold storage are not kept in refrigerators used for domestic purposes but in a separate, designated refrigerator.

C23.6 There is daily monitoring of the temperature of the refrigerator, using a maximum/minimum thermometer, which is recorded and signed by the person monitoring the temperature and a written procedure is in place indicating the action to be taken if the temperature is outside the normal range.

Controlled Drugs

OUTCOME

Controlled drugs are stored, administered and destroyed appropriately.

STANDARD C24

C24.1 Controlled drugs are handled in compliance with the requirements of the Misuse of Drugs Act and its regulations.

C24.2 A hospital that holds stocks of controlled drugs listed in Schedule 2 of the Misuse of Drugs Act has a Home Office licence (unless the hospital is wholly or mainly maintained by voluntary funds or by a registered charity).

C24.3 Where a pharmacist is employed, the purchase and issue of controlled drugs must be under his or her direct supervision and includes authorising orders to suppliers.

C24.4 Where no pharmacist is employed, a medical practitioner or a dentist must countersign orders signed by the registered nurse for a controlled drug.

C24.5 In the case of Schedule 2 controlled drugs (except those in Schedules 4 and 5) an appropriate record is kept of the invoices, receipt, administration and disposal of the drugs in accordance with the Misuse of Drugs Regulations 1985.

C24.6 Controlled drugs are destroyed in the presence of an authorised person (that is a police officer, an inspector of the Home Office Drugs Branch or an inspector of the Royal Pharmaceutical Society of Great Britain), or the person to whom this function has been formally delegated, such as the registered manager or registered nurse of the hospital.

Infection Control

OUTCOME

The risk of patients, staff and visitors acquiring a health care associated infection is minimised.

STANDARD C25

25.1 Key infection control policies are in place, including:

- **universal infection control precautions;**
- **hand hygiene;**
- **prevention of occupational exposure to blood borne viruses(BBVs) and post exposure prophylaxis;**
- **safe handling and disposal of clinical waste;**
- **housekeeping and cleaning regimes for all patient areas;**

- **relevant training and access to advice on infection control; and**
- **occupational health policies for prevention and management of communicable infections in health care workers, including those infected with blood borne viruses.**

Medical Devices and Decontamination

OUTCOME

Patients are not treated with contaminated medical devices.

STANDARD C26

C26.1   Medical devices intended for single use are not reprocessed for reuse.

C26.2   Re-usable medical devices are decontaminated in accordance with legislative and best practice requirements.

Resuscitation

OUTCOME

Patients are resuscitated appropriately.

STANDARD C27

C27.1   There is a written resuscitation policy for the establishment/agency, which is:

- **developed in discussion with (as a minimum) the senior health care professionals;**
- **in line with Resuscitation Council (UK) guidelines;**
- **includes a section on ethical/legal consideration.**

C27.2   The resuscitation policy is brought to the attention of all personnel.

C27.3   There is a member of staff on duty at all times trained in basic resuscitation techniques with up-date training on an annual basis.

C27.4   There is a sensitive exploration of the wishes of competent patients at risk of cardiac or respiratory failure, or with a terminal illness, regarding resuscitation.

Contracts

OUTCOME

Contracts ensure that patients receive goods and services of the appropriate quality.

STANDARD C28

C28.1 **There are written, dated and signed contracts between the establishment/agency and those organisations or individuals with which it contracts for the supply of, or provision to, goods and services.**

C28.2 Contracts include arrangements for the quality monitoring of the services provided under the contract and arrangements to be put in place if the service or goods provided are not of the required quality.

7

Records and Information Management

Introduction to Standards C29 to C31

Effective keeping and handling of records by independent health care providers across the broad range of their business contributes significantly to the efficient provision of treatment and care. It also helps to ensure that treatment and services can be effectively monitored and audited. There are also legal requirements in relation to records and confidential information that these regulations and standards reflect.

Records management relates to the physical management of a record. As such, it includes the data to be recorded, including sufficient data to permit traceability and allow effective audit, for example identifying what instruments used in a particular operation or which medical devices have been implanted. It also includes the security afforded to the records to ensure that confidentiality is safeguarded.

It is important that providers are required to have in place written policies and procedures in respect of all records, record-keeping and the control of documents. We also think it important to specify that arrangements for the storage of records must be secure. Rather than attempt to reiterate the provisions of the Data Protection Act 1998 through these regulations and standards, the standards simply require the provider to reflect in the establishment's records management policy how it will meet the provisions of that Act.

Under the general heading of 'records' we have included a requirement in regulations to keep a register of patients, births, deaths and of all surgical operations. These are provisions carried forward from the Nursing Homes and Mental Nursing Homes Regulations 1984 (regulations 7(1) and 7(2)(a)). The requirement for the NCSC to be notified of a death in an establishment within 24 hours also remains.

Information management relates to the management of the data contained within the records and includes the confidentiality of such data. We regard it as important that the regulated body has written information management policies with which all those who work within the regulated body are familiar. One of the key elements of any such information management policy is the arrangements needed to ensure the confidentiality of patients' health records.

See also, in particular, regulation 21 and Schedule 3 of the Private and Voluntary Health Care Regulations.

Records Management

> **OUTCOME**
>
> Records are created, maintained and stored to standards which meet legal and regulatory compliance and professional practice recommendations.

STANDARD C29

C29.1 **The registered person ensures that there is a records policy for the creation, management, handling, storage and destruction of all records that ensures that records are managed, and stored securely, in accordance with the Data Protection Act 1998.**

C29.2 Any records that are required to be kept under legislation are retained for the relevant periods prescribed in the legislation.

C29.3 Effective back-up arrangements are in place for handling technical breakdown in information systems and to avoid loss or corruption of information held.

C29.4 Destruction of records is undertaken securely.

C29.5 All health records are stored securely with arrangements in place to protect the records from use by unauthorised persons, damage or loss.

C29.6 There is written information that sets out the responsibilities of nominated post-holders for the up dating and safekeeping of records.

Completion of Health Records

> **OUTCOME**
>
> Patients are assured of appropriately completed health records.

STANDARD C30

C30.1 **All entries in patients' health records by health care professionals are dated, timed and signed, with the signature accompanied by the name and designation of the signatory.**

C30.2 All entries in patients' health records are legible.

C30.3 Any alterations or additions are dated, timed and signed, and made in such a way that the original entry can still be read.

C30.4 All health care professionals working on a patient's case record all treatment given and recommendations in the patient's health record.

C30.5   A summary of the patient's health record is sent to the patient's GP within a locally agreed timescale, but which is no more than four weeks.

C30.6   When the referral is not from the patient's GP or dentist, the patient is asked to formally sign a form to give or refuse consent for sending details of the treatment provided (the consultant's discharge letter) to his/her GP.

C30.7   If the patient does not give consent for details to be sent to his/her GP, a summary of the treatment provided is given direct to the patient so that he/she has it for future reference, to pass on to the GP.

Information Management

OUTCOME

Patients are assured that all information is managed within the regulated body to ensure patient confidentiality.

STANDARD C31

C31.1   There is a written information management policy which sets out how the establishment ensures that information held by the establishment on patients, their families and staff is handled confidentially.

C31.2   The information management policy takes account of the:

- Data Protection Act 1998;
- recommendations of the Caldicott Committee report, Report on the review of patient-identifiable information; and
- guidelines from professional bodies.

C31.3   All those who work within the establishment are familiar and comply with the information management policy.

C31.4   There is information for patients on their right to access their health records, in line with The Data Protection Act 1998.

C31.5   There is a written procedure setting out how to respond to patients' requests for access to information in the health record.

C31.6   The establishment submits data, as requested by the National Care Standards Commission to national health care studies and data sets.

8

Research

Introduction to Standard C32

Research is a core component of quality improvement, best value in social care and clinical governance. Research itself must be undertaken within a governance framework. Such a framework has been developed by the Department of Health. This framework sets out standards, delivery mechanisms and monitoring arrangements for all research.

In line with this framework, it is important that if any research is conducted by an independent health care establishment the registered person is responsible for developing and promoting a quality research culture and for ensuring that their staff and those who practice in their premises are supported in, and held to account for, the professional conduct of research.

Organisations that employ researchers, including principal investigators, have responsibility for ensuring that those researchers understand and discharge the responsibilities set out for them in the framework. They should also be prepared to take some or all of the responsibility for ensuring that a study is properly managed and for monitoring its progress. The nature of the responsibilities taken on by the organisation should be agreed with the sponsor who has ultimate responsibility for ensuring that appropriate arrangements are in place for the management and monitoring of any study they sponsor.

The registered person should ensure that agreements are in place between them, their staff, those who practice in their premises, who in turn must have agreements with funders and care organisations, about ownership, exploitation and income from any intellectual property that may arise from research conducted.

All organisations providing health or social care in England must be aware of all research being undertaken in their organisation, or drawing on patient or clients (or their data or tissue) from their organisation. They should ensure that all their patients or users and carers are protected by the attached standard. In particular a research sponsor willing and able to discharge its responsibilities must be identified, and clear and documented agreements must be in place about the allocation of responsibilities between all parties involved. Accountability for this lies with the registered person. The registered person remains responsible for the quality of all aspects of the care of their patients or users, whether or not they are involved in research and whoever that research may be conducted and funded by.

See also, in particular, regulation 24 of the Private and Voluntary Health Care Regulations.

Research

OUTCOME

Any research conducted in the establishment/agency is carried out with appropriate consent and authorisation from any patients involved, in line with published guidance on the conduct of research projects.

STANDARD C32

C32.1 There is a written policy which states whether or not research is carried out in the establishment.

C32.2 Where the policy states that research is carried out within the establishment, there are written procedures that set out the requirements to be met concerning research projects.

C32.3 All clinical research projects are conducted in accordance with the Department of Health research governance framework.

C32.4 Any new interventional procedures to be carried out in the establishment are referred to NICE.

C32.5 All clinical research projects are approved by a Research Ethics Committee.

C32.6 There are documented agreements in place for the allocation of responsibilities between all parties involved.

C32.7 The lead professional for each research project is documented.

C32.8 The responsibilities of the lead professional include:

- the management of the research project;
- the monitoring of progress on the project.

C32.9 There are documented agreements in place between the establishment/agency and their personnel and between the establishment/agency and funders about ownership, exploitation and income from any intellectual property that may arise from research conducted on their premises.

C32.10 Records are kept of all research projects, including information about the patients involved, or patients whose data or tissue has been used in the project, for 15 years after the conclusion of the treatment.

C32.11 Lawful consent or authorisation is obtained for the participation of any patient in a research project.

C32.12 The registered person is responsible for ensuring that all research projects undertaken are appropriate for the organisation to be involved in and are properly managed.

Service-specific Standards

Service-specific Standards

9

Acute Hospitals

Introduction to Standards A1 to A48

These standards apply to:

- establishments where the main purpose of which is to provide medical treatment for illness where one or more overnight beds are provided (subject to certain exceptions, see regulation 3(2)). This includes private hospitals that provide services for NHS patients;
- establishments where medical treatment is provided under anaesthesia or sedation;
- establishments where dental treatment under general anaesthesia takes place; and
- establishments where cosmetic surgery takes place.

The standards cover a variety of procedures, settings and services within acute hospitals, through which a common theme runs: there must be assurance about the quality of the treatment and services that patients receive and appropriate safeguards must be in place. To this end, the key elements throughout the standards are that all those who work within acute hospitals must be suitably qualified, trained and competent, that the right skill mix of workers for particular clinical services is in place, and that safe and appropriate equipment is used.

Information Provision (standards A1 to A2)

Patients should always be given full details of the treatment they are to receive. It is the duty of the clinicians involved to ensure that all patients have an explanation of the likely outcomes of treatment. This is important in connection with cosmetic surgery, where those seeking treatment may be susceptible to unrealistic expectations of what such surgery can achieve. These standards aim to ensure that the patient is given full and clear information about the treatment being proposed before they make their decision on whether to proceed.

See also, in particular, regulation 37 of the Private and Voluntary Health Care Regulations.

Human Resources (standards A3 to A7)

The standards covering human resources aim to ensure that all those who work in the hospital are suitably qualified, trained and competent. They also address more specific issues such as ensuring that appropriate medical cover is available at all times.

See also, in particular, regulations 18 and 19 of the Private and Voluntary Health Care Regulations.

Risk Management (standards A8 to A12)

Health and safety: measures must be in place across the hospital to ensure a safe environment for patients, staff and visitors.

Infection control: prevention and control of infection is part of the overall risk management strategy within the hospital environment, and an integral part of the management of antibiotic resistance.

Decontamination: the decontamination of reusable medical devices is the combination of processes which, if not correctly undertaken, individually or collectively, will increase the likelihood of micro-organisms being transferred to patients or staff. The decontamination process is required to make medical devices safe for use on the patient and safe for members of staff to handle. The reusable medical device life cycle includes acquisition, cleaning, disinfection, inspection, packaging, sterilisation, transportation, and storage before use. This cycle is used to render a reusable item safe for further use.

The Health Technical Memoranda (HTMs) and Health Building Notes (HBNs) referred to in these standards are published by NHS Estates and are available from the Stationery Office. Medical Devices Agency Device Bulletins (MDA-DB) are available from the Medical Devices Agency itself. The European Standards (ENs) are obtainable from the British Standards Institution.

It is anticipated that the NCSC will assess compliance with the decontamination standards in the light of the compliance timetable in the NHS.

Resuscitation: decisions concerning resuscitation are a sensitive area of medical practice. One of the basic principles of health care is that a competent patient has the right under common law to give or withhold consent to examination or treatment. Therefore, when competent patients are at risk of cardiac or respiratory failure, or have a terminal illness, there should be sensitive exploration of their wishes regarding resuscitation.

In the case of patients who are not capable of consenting to treatment, and in the absence of a valid advance refusal of treatment, it is a medical practitioner's duty to act in the best interests of the patient concerned. For some patients this will mean that they should not be subjected to further traumatic or non-beneficial procedures. It is unlawful not to respect a valid advance refusal of treatment made by the patient refusing resuscitation if this is applicable to the circumstances. Decisions about when to resuscitate patients are primarily a clinical matter for the medical practitioner responsible for the treatment of the patient concerned. Before making his or her decision, an assessment is made of the patient's best interests and this assessment should include consultation with other members of the health care team and, where appropriate, family members or others close to the patient.

A decision arrived at in the case of one patient may be inappropriate in a superficially similar case. 'Do not resuscitate' decisions should therefore be reached on a case by case basis. Thus a blanket 'do not resuscitate' policy based on a specific patient group would not be acceptable. The Department of Health's *Resuscitation Policy* (HSC 2000/28) reinforces patients' rights on resuscitation decisions and aims to ensure that patients are properly involved.

See also, in particular, regulations 9 and 35 of the Private and Voluntary Health Care Regulations.

[See: NHS Executive *Controls Assurance Standard Infection Control* (1999); *NHS Executive Controls Assurance Standard Decontamination* (2001).]

Children's Services (standards A13 to A19)

Children are treated relatively infrequently in independent acute hospitals and, apart from hospitals with dedicated paediatric units, should only be admitted for day case or overnight surgical care. Children requiring anaesthesia need specially trained staff and appropriate facilities. Children with pre-existing medical conditions requiring intervention, both acute episodes and planned (elective) intervention, require the comprehensive services of a dedicated paediatric unit, with paediatric medical and paediatric nursing staff on duty at all times, and should not be treated outside these facilities. Children who become unwell, unstable or who develop complications as a result of planned surgery, should be immediately transferred to a paediatric unit. Formal transfer arrangements should be made in advance and defined in policy.

Surgery (standards A20 to A29)

A large amount of the clinical work carried out in independent acute hospitals is surgery. The standards reflect the need for suitably qualified, trained and competent health care professionals, the appropriate equipment, and for documented procedures for operating theatres to be in place in order to ensure that surgical procedures are safe and quality-assured.

Dental surgery under general anaesthesia: in recent years there have been a number of well-publicised deaths, including of children, following general anaesthesia administered for dental treatment. Following a review led by the Chief Medical Officer and Chief Dental Officer, *Department of Health 'A Conscious Decision – a review of the use of general anaesthesia and conscious sedation in primary dental care' (2000),* from 2002 all such general anaesthesia must be provided in a hospital setting with critical care facilities. The standard requires that guidance issued by the Department of Health in connection with this requirement is followed.

Cardiac surgery: some 20% of all coronary bypass surgery takes place in the independent acute sector. For this reason, and because of the specialist nature of this surgery (in respect of the skills of the operator and specialist equipment required), a specific set of standards is included for these procedures.

Cardiac surgery may involve adult, paediatric and neonatal patients and includes all forms of open and closed heart surgery. Coronary revascularisation is a major intervention with risks as well as benefits. It is never undertaken lightly and each and every patient requires careful consideration. The cardiac surgery standards therefore make reference to the standards, set out in the National Service Framework for Coronary Heart Disease, on the numbers of procedures that must be performed annually by the individual trained operator (taking account of the work the individual practitioner carries out both in NHS facilities and in independent hospitals).

Cosmetic plastic surgery: plastic surgery is the general term describing surgery performed to correct a problem caused by other surgery or to create a more pleasing appearance for whatever reason. Cosmetic plastic surgery is the specialisation that focuses on improved appearance for its own sake. It includes procedures such as breast augmentation, face lifts, ear correction, facial implants and fat reduction.

The majority of cosmetic plastic surgery procedures are performed in the independent sector. There is, therefore, a specific set of standards that apply to those procedures. The standards recognising legal complications with requiring all cosmetic surgeons to be on the GMC's specialist register, concentrate on the surgeons demonstrating that they are competent in the procedures they undertake.

Transplantation: most transplantation is carried out in the NHS because of the constraints of organ availability, the huge expense and complexity of the procedures and the resources needed. However, some kidney transplants are undertaken in private hospitals mostly using a related live donor, or cadaver kidneys for which the NHS is unable to find a use.

The standards reflect that transplantation is regulated by the Human Organ Transplants Act 1989. This prohibits commercial dealings in human organs for transplant and restricts the transplanting of organs between people who are not genetically related. The Act also requires information about the removal and the use/disposal of transplanted organs to be sent to the Special Health Authority, UK Transplant.

See also, in particular, regulations 37 and 38 of the Private and Voluntary Health Care Regulations.

[See: Department of Health *Coronary Heart Disease National Service Framework* (2000); Royal College of Anaesthetists *Guidelines for the Provision of Anaesthetic Services* (1999); Royal College of Surgeons *Children's Surgery – A First Class Service* (2000).]

Critical Care (standards A30 to A32)

Some patients in independent acute hospitals may require critical care. Where the hospitals are carrying out complex operations, such as cardiac surgery or transplantation, there must be critical care beds available for patients post-operatively in those hospitals. In other cases, post-operative complications may mean that a patient requires critical care support. The standards provide for the hospital to have made the necessary arrangements so that critical care can be provided as needed in the establishment. Or, that arrangements must be in place with a provider of a higher level of critical care, so that patients can be transferred to appropriate facilities as necessary.

Critical care provision by independent hospitals should be informed by the Department of Health *Review of Adult Critical Care Services* (May 2000).

[See: Department of Health *Comprehensive Critical Care Report* (2000).]

Radiology (standards A33 to A34)

The use of ionising radiation in health care is regulated through a range of legislative measures that implement Euratom Directives to protect employees, the public and patients. This legislation applies equally to the NHS and to the acute independent sector and is enforced by a number of inspectorates including those from the Health and Safety Executive and the Environment Agency. Legislation listed in these standards is that which has a primary impact on patient welfare.

Pharmacy (standards A35 to A42)

These standards concentrate on various key aspects of medicines administration within acute hospitals; responsibility for ordering, handling, disposal etc. of medicines; prescribing and administration of medicines (including self-administration); dealing with adverse incidents; and the storage and supply of medical gasses. They supplement the core standards on Medicines Management (including Controlled Drugs).

Pathology Services (standards A43 to A46)

The quality of pathology services is maintained in three main ways – accreditation of pathology laboratories, state registration of scientific officers and clinical scientists, and underpinning training programmes.

Pathology services may, in whole or in part, be carried out in the hospital, by contract with the laboratory service of a NHS hospital, by contract with another independent hospital or commercial provider or by a combination of these arrangements.

See also, in particular, regulation 34 of the Private and Voluntary Health Care Regulations.

[See: Clinical Pathology Accreditation *Standards for the Medical Laboratory* (2000).]

Cancer Services (standards A47 to A48)

The majority of cancer services are delivered in the NHS but some cancer patients may have part of their course of treatment in independent hospitals. The standards reflect the need for services in the independent sector to reflect the requirements set out in the National Service Framework for cancer services where these relate to chemotherapy and radiotherapy.

[See: Department of Health *The NHS Cancer Plan* (2000).]

Information Provision

Information for Patients

> **OUTCOME**
>
> Patients receive clear information about their treatment.

STANDARD A1

A1.1 **Information materials for patients are written in concise, plain language and explain in non-technical language what the procedure involves and treatment alternatives.**

A1.2 Written information for patients about the relevant surgery or treatment is made available for them to take away after consultation at the hospital

A1.3 The written information given at the consultation includes general and procedure-specific risks and complications associated with the surgery or other treatment.

A1.4 Documented post-operative instructions are given to patients to take home after the procedure/operation.

A1.5 Patient information materials are agreed by the registered person before being published and made available to patients.

Advertising

> **OUTCOME**
>
> Patients are not misled by advertisements about the hospital and the treatments it provides.

STANDARD A2

A2.1 **All advertising complies with Advertising Standards Authority standards.**

A2.3 Promotional events such as open evenings do not include financial incentives for potential patients to book a consultation appointment at the event.

A2.4 All staff and speakers at promotional events are to be clearly identified with regard to their profession and role within the organisation.

Human Resources

Qualifications of All Medical Practitioners

OUTCOME

Patients receive investigation and treatment from appropriately trained, qualified and insured medical practitioners.

STANDARD A3

A3.1 **All medical practitioners (ie including medical practitioners undertaking independent private practice whether employed, contracted or self-employed providing health screening or resident medical officer services on behalf of and as part of the hospital) are registered with the General Medical Council as medical practitioners.**

A3.2 All medical practitioners have annual appraisals and are revalidated in line with GMC requirements.

A3.3 All medical practitioners are covered by appropriate professional indemnity insurance *either* as specifically identified employees of the hospital through the policies of insurance maintained by the hospital *or* as members of a medical defence organisation approved by the hospital and its insurers.

A3.4 All medical practitioners provide the registered person with, and make available to the National Care Standards Commission, the following clinical and performance indicators about any patient they have treated:

- any deaths at the hospital;
- unplanned re-admissions to hospital;
- unplanned returns to theatre;
- unplanned transfers to other hospitals;
- adverse clinical incidents;
- incidence of post-operative deep vein thrombosis;
- post operative infection rates for the hospital.

Qualifications and Experience of Medical Practitioners Undertaking Independent Private Practice (ie without supervision, commonly known as "Consultants")

> **OUTCOME**
>
> Medical practitioners who work independently in private practice are competent in the procedures they undertake and the treatment and services they provide.

STANDARD A4

A4.1 **Medical practitioners who work independently in private practice:**

- **clearly demonstrate that they have the necessary qualifications, expertise and experience to undertake competently and safely the treatment and services they provide; and**

- **have arrangements in place for continuing medical education relevant to the treatment and services they provide.**

A4.2 Medical practitioners who work independently in private practice (except GPs):

- are on the specialist register of the General Medical Council; *or*

- where they were undertaking cosmetic surgery in the independent health care sector before 1 April 2002 and are not on the specialist register, satisfy the following conditions:

  - have completed recognised basic surgical or medical training;

  - have undertaken specialist training in a speciality relevant to the procedures they provide;

  - maintain a record of patients to whom they have provided treatment or services in the establishment, which is made available to the registered person and to the National Care Standards Commission;

  - undertake regular patient satisfaction surveys, a record of which is made available to the registered person and the National Care Standards Commission at least annually.

A4.3 Medical practitioners undertaking cosmetic surgery independently in private practice for the first time from 1 April 2002 are on the specialist register of the General Medical Council.

Practising Privileges and the Medical Advisory Committee

OUTCOME

Patients receive treatment from medical practitioners who have the appropriate expertise.

STANDARD A5

A5.1 **Where medical practitioners are granted practising privileges there is a medical advisory committee for the hospital, which is responsible for representing the professional needs and views of medical practitioner to the registered manager of the hospital.**

A5.2 The medical advisory committee meets quarterly as a minimum and formal minutes are kept of meetings.

A5.3 The medical advisory committee makes recommendations to the registered manager on:

- eligibility criteria for practising privileges;
- each application for practising privileges;
- the review and possible suspension, restriction or withdrawal of practising privileges;
- the introduction of new clinical techniques to the hospital, including the training requirements for medical practitioners to undertake the technique, the equipment required and the training/experience required by other clinical staff to support the technique(s).

A5.4 The medical advisory committee reviews twice per year as a minimum, information collated on the clinical work undertaken at the hospital by all practitioners with practising privileges by specialty, procedure and by clinical responsibility, to include as a minimum:

- any deaths at the hospital;
- unplanned re-admissions to hospital;
- unplanned returns to theatre;
- unplanned transfers to other hospitals;
- adverse clinical incidents;
- incidence of post-operative deep vein thrombosis;
- post-operative infection rates for the hospital.

Resident Medical Officers

> **OUTCOME**
>
> Patients have an appropriately skilled and trained doctor available to them at all times within the hospital.

STANDARD A6

A6.1 **Where the establishment provides in-patient care there is a resident medical officer available on immediate call at all times to manage urgent patient care in the absence of the consultant under whom the patient is admitted.**

A6.2 Resident medical officers have post-registration clinical experience relevant to the clinical work undertaken in the hospital.

A6.3 Resident medical officers undertake a formal induction programme, the content of which is documented.

A6.4 Resident medical officers undertake resuscitation training to Advanced Life Support level, including defibrillation and intubation skills, on appointment which is up-dated annually.

A6.5 Where the hospital admits children the resident medical officer is trained in Paediatric Advanced Life Support, which is up-dated annually.

A6.6 There is written job description for the resident medical officer, which includes the line management arrangements for the post and the hours on-call and shift patterns.

A6.7 Resident medical officers have access to advice and support at all times from medical consultants with practising privileges and the communication arrangements are documented.

A6.8 The accommodation for resident medical officers, while on-call, is sited within easy reach of the areas in which patients are cared for.

A6.9 The resident medical officer's on-call accommodation has a telephone connected to the hospital's internal telephone system.

Allied Health Professions

OUTCOME

Patients receive treatment from appropriately skilled and qualified members of the allied health professions.

STANDARD A7

A7.1 **Patients requiring consultation with, or treatment from, a member of one of the allied health professions are seen by a practitioner who is registered with the Health Professions Council.**

A7.2 Practitioners registered with the Health Professions Council comply with their professional body's code of practice/rules of professional conduct and standards of practice/care in consulting with and treating patients.

A7.3 There are written policies for the arrangements for out-of-hours cover for appropriate allied health professionals.

A7.4 Members of the allied health professions work as members of a multi-professional team caring for patients.

A7.5 Allied health professionals participate in multi-professional activities such as case conferences, ward rounds and individual patient care meetings.

A7.6 Each patient referred to allied health professionals has a care plan for the treatment to be delivered.

Training, Experience and Qualifications of Staff

OUTCOME

Patients receive treatment from appropriately qualified and trained staff.

STANDARD A8

A8.1 **The registered person ensures that healthcare professionals are qualified and trained for the roles they undertake.**

A8.2 Resuscitation training, including annual up-date, is mandatory for all clinical staff, and is in line with current Resuscitation Council (UK) publications.

A8.3 Simulation exercises are undertaken to familiarise staff with emergency care.

A8.4   Nurses delegated to carry out procedures on behalf of a medical practitioner are indemnified for this and trained in the techniques, and deem themselves competent to undertake these procedures in accordance with the of Nurses & Midwives Council (NMC) scope of professional practice.

A8.5   Health care professionals undertake on-going education in the techniques and skills relevant to the clinical area in which they work and the procedures they are undertaking.

A8.6   All healthcare professionals using equipment must have completed training in the safe clinical use of the equipment, records of which are documented.

A8.7   All clinical staff undertake continuous professional development and demonstrate that they meet the requirements for professional registration, such as revalidation.

A8.8   There is a programme of ongoing education for all staff, including update of policies, feedback of audit results and action needed to correct deficiencies.

A8.9   Education and training in infection control and decontamination is provided to all health care staff, including those employed in support services.

A8.10   Infection control is included in induction programmes for new staff, including support service staff.

Risk Management

Health and Safety

OUTCOME

Patients, staff and anyone visiting the hospital are assured that all steps are taken to ensure the safety of the hospital environment through the ongoing assessment and management of risks, in relation to all the hospital's activities.

STANDARD A9

A9.1   An annual health and safety report is produced by the hospital. The report summarises the actions taken to ensure a safe, healthy environment, including, for example, training given to staff, risk assessments undertaken and action taken as a result, and an outline plan for health and safety actions to be implemented in the year ahead.

Infection Control

OUTCOME

The risk of patients, staff and visitors acquiring a health care associated infection is minimised.

STANDARD A10

A10.1 **There is an infection control team (ICT), either within the hospital or in another organisation to which the hospital has formal links and membership of the infection control team of that organisation.**

A10.2   The membership of the ICT includes:

- an infection control doctor (ICD);

- an infection control nurse; and

- a consultant medical microbiologist if the ICD is from another speciality.

A10.3   There is a registered nurse with designated responsibilities for infection control included in a documented job description and there is a defined time commitment for infection control activities.

A10.4   The infection control link nurse has training in infection control and provides evidence of continuing professional development (CPD) in relation to the role in infection control.

A10.5   The infection control link nurse liases closely with the occupational health service when dealing with:

- infection control advice relating to the health and safety of health care workers; and

- infection control advice relating to the transmission of infection from health care workers to patients or other members of the organisation's staff and visitors.

A10.6   The infection control link nurse liases with the local consultant in communicable disease control when dealing with outbreaks within the hospital.

A10.7   Prevention and control of infection are considered as part of all service development activity.

A10.8   Infection control advice is available, particularly in relation to the following:

- the development of policies relating to engineering and building services for the hospital and to the purchase of medical devices/equipment, including early stage planning; and

- all stages of the contracting process for services, which have implications for infection control, for example, housekeeping, laundry, clinical waste.

A10.9　Written policies, procedures and guidance for the prevention and control of infection are implemented and reflect relevant legislation and published professional guidance, including:

- major outbreaks of communicable infections;
- isolation of patients;
- antimicrobial prescribing;
- control of MRSA, VRE and other antimicrobial resistant micro-organisms;
- control of tuberculosis, including multi-drug resistant tuberculosis;
- collection, packaging, handling and delivery of laboratory specimens;
- handling of medical devices in procedures carried out on known/suspect CJD patients and on patients in risk categories for CJD as defined in the ACDP/SEAC guidance (including disposal/quarantining procedures).

A10.10　Each department or service has a current copy of the approved policies, procedures and guidelines pertinent to its activities.

A10.11　The infection control link nurse has access to up-to-date legislation and guidance relevant to infection control.

A10.12　Specialist microbiological support is provided for the infection control service, including the interpretation of results, either on-site or via reference centres.

A10.13　The microbiology laboratory used supports the infection control service via processing, data provision, surveillance and specialist testing.

Decontamination

OUTCOME

Patients are not infected by contaminated medical devices.

STANDARD A11

A11.1　Clear lines of accountability for all parts of the decontamination cycle are established.

A11.2　The lines of accountability include contractors and professional liability where the organisation either buys in or sells services to other organisations.

A11.3　An annual report on the efficacy of the decontamination process is submitted to senior management.

A11.4　Written policies and procedures define, document and control all stages of the decontamination process.

A11.5　The written policies and procedures are available for all personnel involved in any aspect of decontamination.

A11.6 All personnel involved in decontamination processes have access to up-to-date legislation and guidance.

A11.7 All contaminated reusable medical devices are handled, collected and transported to the decontamination area in a manner that avoids the risk of contamination to patients, personnel and any area of the health care facility.

A11.8 Personnel are trained to handle, collect and transport contaminated medical devices/equipment safely and wear protective clothing in accordance with local safety policies and procedures.

A11.9 Cleaning, disinfection, storage and use of flexible or rigid endoscopes are undertaken in accordance with MDA DB 9607.

A11.10 Reusable medical devices are reprocessed in a sterile service department.

A11.11 There is a documented traceability system which covers all items sterilised within the hospital.

A11.12 Devices are cleaned in accordance with the manufacturer's instructions.

A11.13 Mechanical washer-disinfectors are specified, commissioned and monitored in accordance with BS 2745 and HTM 2030.

A11.14 Detergents are used in accordance with material safety data sheets.

A11.15 Sterile service department sterilizers are validated, maintained and managed according to HTM 2010 and HTM 2031.

A11.16 Porous load steam sterilizers conform to EN 285: 1997 Sterilization – Steam Sterilizers – Large Sterilizers.

A11.17 A benchtop steam sterilizer is used only in exceptional circumstances, is suitable for the intended loads, and is validated, maintained and operated in accordance with the manufacturer's instructions.

A11.18 There is a post sterilization drying stage if sterilized items are to be stored for future use, which includes the inspection of packages and wrapped items to ensure that they are dry when they are removed from the sterilizer

A11.19 Manual cleaning is only undertaken in unavoidable circumstances and there is a written procedure to be followed.

A11.20 Ethylene oxide sterilizer installations meet HBN 13 Supplement 1. Ethylene oxide sterilizers are validated, maintained and managed according to HTM 2010.

A11.21 Personnel are exposed to ethylene oxide for as short a time as possible and in no circumstances exceed the maximum exposure time limits set out in Schedule 1 of the Control of Substances Hazardous to Health (COSHH) Regulations.

A11.22 All medical devices, decontamination equipment and surfaces used on a patient known to have or suspected of having CJD, or in a risk category for CJD, are dealt with in accordance with guidance published in (ACDP/SEAC) and HSC *Transmissible Spongiform Encephalopathy Agents. Safe Working and the Prevention of Infection* (1999/178).

A11.23 Every location in which the decontamination of reusable medical devices is carried out meets the standards set out DH guidance (eg HTM 2010, HTM 2030 and HBN 13) and includes the conditions defined in all relevant Statutory advice including MDD Registration 93/42/EEC, Health and Safety at Work Act 1974 and Consumer Protection Act 1987.

A11.24 Sterile service department facilities are designed to allow the segregation of clean and dirty activities.

A11.25 All personnel entering and leaving the clean production area:

- do so through a dedicated entrance/exit;
- thoroughly wash and dry hands on entry and exit;
- wear appropriate clothing whilst in the area.

Resuscitation

OUTCOME

Patients are resuscitated appropriately.

STANDARD A12

A12.1 **The registered person ensures that patients' rights are central to decision making on resuscitation, including taking account of advance directives (living wills).**

A12.2 The resuscitation policy makes specific reference to the decision-making and management of 'do not resuscitate' situations for critically ill patients.

A12.3 There is a written procedure for the steps to be undertaken in reaching a decision to withdraw treatment.

A12.4 All 'Do not resuscitate' decisions are documented, with the reason and date for review in the patient's health record.

A12.5 The policy includes appropriate supervision arrangements to review resuscitation decisions.

A12.6 Healthcare professionals with a thorough understanding of the resuscitation policy and its application are on duty at all times and available to make resuscitation decisions.

A12.7 There is at least one person with Advanced Life Support (ALS) training, which is subject to annual up-dating, on duty at all times. This may be the RMO.

A12.8 Where children are admitted for treatment there is at least one person with Paediatric Advanced Life Support (PALS) training, which is up-dated annually, on duty at all times. This may be the RMO. (for child in-patients see A14.11)

A12.9 Resuscitation drills are practised once every two months together by members of the emergency resuscitation team.

A12.10 Induction and staff development programmes cover the resuscitation policy.

A12.11 Clinical practice in the area of resuscitation and the operation of the resuscitation policy is audited at least every three years.

Resuscitation Equipment

OUTCOME

Appropriate resuscitation equipment is in place.

STANDARD A13

A13.1 Resuscitation equipment is readily available.

A13.2 Equipment for resuscitating patients includes:

- a defibrillator;
- portable oxygen with appropriate valves, mask, metering and delivery system;
- first line resuscitation drugs
- equipment for maintaining and securing the airway of a patient

    and

- that necessary to insert and maintain intravenous infusions.

A13.3 Resuscitation equipment is checked and restocked to ensure all equipment remains in working order and suitable for use at all times, and checks are recorded with the person's signature. Checks are carried out daily.

A13.4 Resuscitation equipment is cleaned and decontaminated after each usage, including practice use.

A13.5 A written record is kept of the resuscitation equipment to be kept available in each area of the establishment.

A13.6 Resuscitation equipment is easily accessible and personnel are aware of its location.

A13.7 During induction all personnel are made aware of the location of the resuscitation equipment.

Children's Services

Meeting the Psychological and Social Needs of Children

OUTCOME

The non-clinical needs of children are recognised and addressed.

STANDARD A14

A14.1 **There is a pre-planned programme and the opportunity for a pre-admission visit to allay anxiety on the part of the child.**

A14.2 There is information, specifically written for children and young people about their treatment and care in the hospital.

A14.3 The special needs of, and specific services for, children from different ethnic, cultural or religious backgrounds are reflected in local policies, as appropriate to the patient population.

A14.4 Children are kept in hospital only if their needs cannot be met at home, and they are discharged as soon as possible.

Staff Qualifications, Training and Availability to Meet the Needs of Children

OUTCOME

Children receive treatment from appropriately trained and qualified health care professionals.

STANDARD A15

A15.1 **There is a written admission policy for children, which identifies the criteria for paediatric admissions for which the hospital has the relevant services, facilities and trained personnel.**

A15.2 There is at least one registered nurse who holds a qualification in the care of sick children, either a Registered Sick Children's Nurse (RSCN) or Registered Nurse (RN) Child Branch certificate, on duty at times when children under the age of 12 are being treated or cared for.

A15.3 Where the hospital operates a separate children's department or ward, there are at least two such qualified nurses on duty at all times.

A15.4   Children under three years of age are only accepted in a unit with children's nurses, holding one of the above qualifications and paediatric medical staff on duty at all times during the admission of the child.

A15.5   Links with other children's nurses either within the independent sector or with local NHS providers are encouraged and educational programme opportunities are developed and shared.

A15.6   The qualified children's nurse is responsible for planning the child's nursing care needs and completing a written record of the care plan, and for negotiating routine care with the family.

A15.7   Surgical lists to include children under the age of 12, or adolescents under the age of 16, are planned in consultation with the senior registered nurse to ensure that qualified children's nurses are on-duty on the appropriate shifts.

A15.8   A lead children's nurse is responsible for policies and protocols that are child based and family friendly, and audits paediatric care in line with the policies and protocols on a regular basis.

A15.9   Children under the age of three who carry additional surgical and anaesthesia risks are only cared for by surgeons and anaesthetists experienced in the clinical care of young children and by registered children's nurses.

A15.10 Surgeons, anaesthetists and other staff do not undertake acute paediatric procedures only on an occasional basis, and services must comply with guidance issued by the Paediatric Forum of The Royal College of Surgeons of England *Children's Surgery – A First Class Service* (May 2000).

A15.11 Every child is placed under the care of a named consultant.

A15.12 In addition, when children are admitted as in-patients there is a resident medical officer on duty at all times who has a minimum of six months recent paediatric experience and an accredited Paediatric Advanced Life Support certificate.

A15.13 Anaesthesia for children under the age of 12 is provided by an anaesthetist with specialist training in paediatric anaesthesia.

A15.14 There is a nominated lead consultant responsible for the oversight and organisation of all anaesthesia services for children in the hospital, including pain and resuscitation services, and for ensuring that suitable equipment, including paediatric resuscitation equipment, is purchased and maintained.

A15.15 Registered nurses and operating department practitioners with paediatric training are available at all times to assist the anaesthetist.

A15.16 Recovery staff have training and experience to ensure safe post-operative care of children.

Facilities and Equipment to Meet the Needs of Children

> **OUTCOME**
>
> Children's treatment is provided with the appropriate facilities and equipment.

STANDARD A16

A16.1 Children are seen in a separate outpatient area, or where the hospital does not have a separate outpatient area for children they are seen promptly.

A16.2 The outpatient area is subject to the same environmental audit as any other area used for children to ensure that the area is safe, with any identified risks to children controlled.

A16.3 Toys and/or books suitable to the child's age are provided.

A16.4 Children requiring anaesthesia or sedation are admitted to a bed and not treated in outpatients.

A16.5 All children are admitted to a single room or to one shared with other children only. An environmental risk assessment is performed to ensure the child's safety.

A16.6 Children under the age of 12 are supervised in their rooms at all times either by hospital staff or by their parents.

A16.7 On admission children are carefully weighed with minimal clothing to allow for accurate calculation of drugs. Dual checking is recommended for the weighing of small children.

A16.8 There are segregated areas for the reception of children and adolescents into theatre and for recovery, to screen the children and adolescents from adult patients; the segregated areas contain all necessary equipment for the care of children.

A16.9 A parent is to be actively encouraged to stay at all times, with accommodation made available for the adult in the child's room or close by.

A16.10 The child's family is allowed to visit him/her at any time of the day, except when in individual circumstances a decision is made by the clinical team that visiting should be restricted.

A16.11 Adolescents are to have their privacy respected, and every effort is made to respect their wishes if they indicate they prefer to be seen without their parents.

A16.12 The toys provided are safe (compliant with British Safety Standards), and are age appropriate to the child.

A16.13 When a child is in hospital for more than five days, play is managed and supervised by a qualified Hospital Play Specialist.

A16.14 Children are required to receive education when in hospital for more than five days; the Local Education Authority has an obligation to meet this need and are contacted if necessary.

Meeting Children's Needs During Surgery

OUTCOME

Children receive appropriate treatment in connection with surgery.

STANDARD A17

A17.1 **Prior to surgery, children are left without food or drink for as short a time as possible, in consultation with the anaesthetist.**

A17.2 Clear fluids are not withheld for more than two or three hours prior to surgery.

A17.3 The use of pre-medications, and intra-muscular injections in particular, in minor or day case surgery is exceptional and these are recorded.

A17.4 Verbal consent for *per rectum* medication is obtained when general anaesthesia is being given and is recorded in the child's health record.

A17.5 The child is subjected to the least amount of pain as possible prior to cannulation, through the use of local anaesthetic cream.

A17.6 Where child exclusive lists are not used, children and adolescents are operated on at the beginning of the list to assess starvation times accurately and to avoid contact with adult patients.

A17.7 The child's named nurse and a parent accompany the child to theatre. The parent(s) is given the option of being present until the child is asleep.

A17.8 A children's nurse collects the child, if under the age of 12, from the recovery area. The parent(s) is given the option of accompanying the child from the recovery area.

Pain Management for Children

OUTCOME

Children receive appropriate pain control.

STANDARD A18

A18.1 **There are written procedures for the assessment of pain in children and the provision of appropriate control.**

A18.2 A child's pain is assessed in partnership with the family, who know what is normal behaviour for their child, and by using a recognised pain assessment tool.

A18.3   Analgesia is given by an appropriate route, avoiding the intramuscular route.

A18.4   Provision is made for adequate analgesia on discharge of the child, in discussion with the family.

Transfer of Children

OUTCOME

In emergencies, children are transferred quickly and safely to paediatric units.

STANDARD A19

A19.1   There is a written policy for a child who becomes unwell, or unstable, or who develops complications as a result of planned surgery, to be immediately transferred to a paediatric unit.

A19.2   Contingency emergency transfer arrangements are documented and agreed in advance with the paediatric unit.

A19.3   All staff caring for children are trained in paediatric resuscitation.

A19.4   Paediatric resuscitation equipment is separate from the adult equipment and the same system used for wards and theatres.

A19.5   Simulation exercises are undertaken to familiarise staff with emergency paediatric care.

Surgery

Documented Procedures for Surgery – General

OUTCOME

Patients are assured that effective procedures for surgery are in place.

STANDARD A20

A20.1   There are written policies and procedures for the carrying out of surgical operations, covering staffing arrangements, equipment, installations, facilities and theatre practice.

A20.2   There are written policies and procedures for preventing venous thromboembolism.

A20.3   A system is in place to identify a formal planned schedule of operating sessions for elective surgery, which includes a system of inter-disciplinary consultation when changes to schedules are required. In addition, the theatre manager has the right of veto.

A20.4   There are written procedures for:

- patient identification;

- verification and site of the operation;

- checking for pre-operative preparation of skin, false teeth and crowns;

- checking pre-operative tests such as radiographs, ECGs and others as may be required.

A20.5   There are written procedures for the counting of items such as swabs, needles, operative instruments and blades, and what to do if items cannot be accounted for.

A20.6   There are written policies & procedures to ensure that surgeons comply   with   the National Joint Registry.

A20.7   The full details, including batch numbers and/or serial numbers, of all implanted medical devices are recorded in the patient's individual records and on a master list held in the operating theatre department. A copy of this information is passed to the patient.

A20.8   Entries in the surgical register are validated as follows:

- a person is nominated to enter information in the register and signs it to confirm that the entries are accurate;

- the nurse responsible for checking swabs, needles and equipment signs the register;

- a secondary checking of swabs, needles and equipment is undertaken and the register is signed by the person carrying out those checks.

Documented Procedures for Surgery – Patient Care

OUTCOME

The procedures for surgery assure patients of safe and effective treatment.

STANDARD A21

A21.1   All surgery patients have a pre-admission appointment with the surgeon/ practitioner who will be carrying out the procedure.

A21.2   There are written pre-operative policies and procedures, which include unambiguous instructions to patients on:

- fasting;

- medication;

- escorts;

- transport arrangements;

- contact details for patient's queries, such as telephone and fax numbers and e-mail address.

A21.3   There are written policies and procedures for assessing the patient's fitness for treatment, including:

- how pre-operative medical condition(s) are brought to the attention of both the anaesthetist and surgeon;

- how the patient's medical practitioner is consulted prior to the date of the procedure being undertaken.

A21.4   Pre-operative medical condition(s) are recorded.

A21.5   The person undertaking the surgical procedure ensures that the patient has given valid consent for the proposed surgery and/or anaesthesia and ensures the relevant consent forms are signed.

A21.6   There are written pre-operative procedures covering:

- the appropriate positioning of the patient on the operating table

- the protection of the patient from diathermy burns

- the protection of the patient from laser and radiation risks, as appropriate.

A21.7   There are written post-operative policies and procedures, which include instructions for the patient on:

- pain relief;

- bleeding;

- care of the post-operative site;

- how the effects of general anaesthesia may impair their judgement and that they should refrain from certain activities such as driving, operating machinery or signing legal documents;

- a telephone contact number at the hospital.

A21.8   There are written policies for discharge which require:

- that an appropriate medical practitioner is responsible for discharging the patient;

- procedures for assessing the patient's fitness for discharge and the criteria for that decision;

- the discharged patient to be accompanied home by a responsible adult.

A21.9   There are written procedures for staff to follow when requesting donor organs from the family members of a deceased patient.

A21.10 Staff are trained in how to approach family members with regard to organ donation.

Anaesthesia and Recovery

OUTCOME

Patients receive the appropriate level of care when receiving surgical treatment.

STANDARD A22

A22.1 The anaesthetist who is to give the anaesthetic visits the patient before the operation and assesses the general medical fitness of the patient, reviews any medication being taken, and assesses any specific anaesthesia problems.

A22.2 The anaesthetist discusses possible plans of management with the patient and explains any options available, to enable the patient to make an informed choice.

A22.3 Information on any drugs or treatments such as blood transfusion to be given while under general anaesthesia is discussed with the patient.

A22.4 The anaesthetist documents the choice of anaesthetic technique and the post-operative management and the anaesthetic assessment in the patient's health record.

A22.5 The anaesthetist ensures that all the necessary equipment and drugs are present and checked before starting anaesthesia.

A22.6 The anaesthetist confirms the identity of the patient before inducing anaesthesia.

A22.7 The anaesthetist is present in the operating theatre throughout the operation and is present on-site until the patient has been discharged from the recovery room.

A22.8 The conduct of the anaesthesia and operation is monitored and recorded in line with the minimum monitoring standards document of the Association of Anaesthetists for Great Britain and Ireland:

- by a continuous display of the ECG;
- pulse oximetry
- arterial pressure must be recorded, at a minimum of 5 minute intervals;
- where the patient breathes an artificial gas mixture, the inspired oxygen concentration is measured;
- a written or printed record of the anaesthetic is kept as a permanent record in the case notes.

A22.9 Until patients regain full consciousness following anaesthesia and surgery they are closely observed on a one-to-one basis by staff trained in recovery room procedures and resuscitation.

A22.10 Pain is assessed in discussion with the patient and pain control provided.

A22.11 Unless patients require transfer for level 2 or level 3 critical care they are managed in a recovery room.

A22.12 The recovery room is sited within the operating department and away from the admission area to the department, and conforms to Department of Health and Association of Anaesthetists guidelines in respect of design and levels of equipment.

A22.13 The recovery room:

- has monitoring equipment, including ECG;

- has resuscitation equipment including a defibrillator;

- is of sufficient size to accommodate a patient resting in a recumbent position, staff and resuscitation equipment;

- ensures ease of communication and access for staff in the event of an accident or emergency.

A22.14 There is one person on duty in the operating theatre at all times with certified training in advanced life support.

A22.15 Clinical observation notes recording the patient's progress are kept in the case notes including for example the patient's respiratory state, cardiac system and skin condition.

A22.16 Written discharge criteria are in place, including satisfactory control of pain and nausea, to determine when patients can be safely discharged from the recovery room, making it clear that the final responsibility is always with the anaesthetist who administered the anaesthesia.

Operating Theatres

OUTCOME

Operating theatres have appropriate facilities, equipment, support services and staffing arrangements.

STANDARD A23

A23.1 Operating theatres have available instruments and equipment from a sterile services unit.

A23.2 There is an emergency power supply for the operating theatre, in accordance with S.I.1984/1578, regulation 12(2)(b), to provide electrical power in the event of an interruption to the mains supply.

A23.3 Full equipment for endotracheal intubation is available to hand. There is immediate access to spare apparatus in the event of failure.

A23.4 There is appropriate and effective suction apparatus which is independently powered and portable.

A23.5 When artificial ventilation equipment is used, a disconnect alarm is used.

A23.6 Support services are provided, including pathology and radiology.

A23.7   Arrangements for the staffing and management of an operating suite are in line with published professional guidance for the operation taking place.

A23.8   There are written descriptions for the role of each member of professional staff in the operating theatre (including visiting staff), which include the allocation of responsibility for management and a description of the role for:

- medical practitioners;
- registered nurses;
- care assistants;
- operating department practitioners;
- blood perfusionists and specialist technical staff.

A23.9   A registered nurse or operating department practitioner who has operating theatre experience is in charge at all times in the operating theatre.

A23.9   The operating area is of sufficient size to accommodate the patient, their escort, the anaesthetist, the surgeon and the assistants for the anaesthetist and the surgeon.

Procedures and Facilities Specific to Dental Treatment under General Anaesthesia Facilities

OUTCOME

Patients are assured of safe and effective dental treatment under general anaesthesia.

STANDARD 24

A24.1   Establishments carrying out dental surgery under general anaesthesia meet the Department of Health, General Dental Council and Royal College of Anaesthetists guidance with regard to procedures and facilities.

Cardiac Surgery

OUTCOME

Cardiac surgery only takes place in hospitals that have the appropriate facilities and expertise to do so.

STANDARD A25

A25.1   Cardiac surgery must take place in operating rooms fully equipped for cardiothoracic surgery.

A25.2   The registered person has regard to the facility and operator standards for angiography, PTCA and CABG in the NHS National Service Framework for Coronary Heart Disease determining the adequacy of the skills and experience of individual operators and teams engaged in this work. The experience and number of cases carried out may be combined from work in both the NHS and independent sector.

A25.3   There is a consultant anaesthetist with responsibility for cardiac anaesthesia services.

A25.4   Haematology, blood transfusion and biochemistry services are available within rapid access.

A25.5   Satellite laboratory services are in or near the operating room for the measurement of blood gases, electrolytes, haemoglobin and anticoagulation.

A25.6   Patient monitoring equipment and heart by-pass machines are maintained, repaired and calibrated by medical physicists or other suitably qualified technicians, or maintained by contractual arrangement with an external supplier, with documents available to confirm this.

A25.7   Critical care at level 2 at a minimum is provided on site in which patients can be nursed immediately after the operation.

A25.8   Audit of cardiac surgery is undertaken in line with the Society of Cardiothoracic Surgeons of Great Britain and Ireland, and the British Cardiovascular Intervention Society/British Cardiac Society. This may be in conjunction with audit programmes in NHS trusts.

A25.9   Audit data is shared for peer review purposes; this may be through an associated clinical audit programme at a NHS trust.

A25.10 Agreed protocols/systems of care are in place so that, prior to discharge from hospital, people admitted suffering from coronary heart disease are invited to participate in a multi-disciplinary programme of secondary prevention and cardiac rehabilitation.

A25.11 Assessment of physical, psychological and social needs for cardiac rehabilitation is carried out before discharge.

A25.12 A written individual plan for meeting these identified needs is prepared and copied to the patient and his/her GP.

A25.13 Initial advice on lifestyle, for example smoking cessation, physical activity (including sexual activity), diet, alcohol consumption and employment is provided and recorded.

A25.14 Information about cardiac support groups is provided.

A25.15 Locally relevant information about cardiac rehabilitation is provided.

Cosmetic Surgery

OUTCOME

Patients are clear as to what cosmetic surgery entails, and are assured about the skills and experience of those carrying out those procedures.

STANDARD A26

A26.1 **Surgeons performing cosmetic surgery procedures belong to a relevant professional organisation, which provides continuing medical education and adheres to the principles of the GMC's *Good Medical Practice*.**

A26.2 All surgeons maintain a comprehensive outpatient service, either at the clinic/hospital where the surgery is to be undertaken or elsewhere, ensuring that the surgeon has assessed and documented in the patient's health record the patient's appropriateness for receiving cosmetic surgery.

A26.3 No patient is admitted for the procedure the same day as the initial consultation.

A26.4 Referral to appropriate psychological counselling is available if clinically indicated prior to surgery.

A26.5 There are dated, documented criteria which set out the risk factors associated with the individual procedures and guide the selection of patients for different treatment options. These are held by the surgeon and discussed with the patient prior to surgery.

A26.6 There are written procedures for the safe use of all equipment used for cosmetic surgery purposes within the hospital.

A26.7 All staff using equipment have completed training in the safe clinical use of the equipment and have demonstrated competence, which is documented to this effect.

Day Surgery

OUTCOME

Patients undergoing day surgery receive appropriate treatment and support, including the pre and post-operative periods

STANDARD A27

A27.1 **There are procedures for appropriate patient selection for day case surgery. These include consideration of social factors such as whether the patient lives alone or has someone available to stay with them.**

A27.2 Access is available to clinical support services: radiology, pharmacy, investigative laboratories.

A27.3   Access to inpatient beds is available for post-operative complications requiring an overnight stay.

A27.4   All patients are assessed during the recovery phase for the adequacy of analgesia and fitness for discharge.

A27.5   Specific instructions are available for patients, their relatives and community services if appropriate. Post-operative information must be provided for patients specific to each procedure undertaken in a day surgical unit, for example lens extraction, hernia, grommets.

Transplantation

OUTCOME
Transplantation takes place safely and sensitively.

STANDARD A28

A28.1   The requirements of the Human Organs Transplants Act 1989 are complied with.

A28.2   There are written policies and procedures for the conduct of transplantation operations to ensure the traceability of all donor organs that prohibit the purchase or sale of any human organs for transplant in whatever way and from whatever source.

A28.3   The procedures ensure that transplantation of organs between living people who are not genetically related is not carried out without the prior permission of the Unrelated Live Transplant Regulatory Authority.

A28.4   Information about organs removed for proposed transplants and about organs which have been transplanted into other persons is reported in accordance with the Human Organs Transplants (Supply of Information) Regulations 1989.

A28.5   In participating in the national scheme for the allocation of organs, all patients are registered on a national waiting list and follow-up information on transplanted patients is provided for inclusion on the National Transplant Database.

A28.6   There are written policies and procedures for xenotransplantation operations, which are in accordance with published guidance and have been scrutinised and approved by the UK Xenotransplantation Interim Regulatory Authority.

A28.7   There are documented, defined criteria and processes for the selection of suitable patients for transplantation and these are monitored.

A28.8   Critical care at level 3 is provided on site for nursing patients immediately after the operation.

A28.9   Records are kept for 11 years from the date of discharge or death of the patient.

Critical Care

Arrangements for immediate critical care

OUTCOME

Appropriate post-operative and emergency arrangements are in place for patients who undergo surgery.

STANDARD A29

A29.1 **There are level 1 critical care facilities available for patients who have received treatment under general anaesthetic and require:**

- **frequent observation by nursing staff;**
- **frequent or continuous cardiovascular monitoring;**
- **high risk intravenous infusions, for example anti-arrhythmic, vasodilators or inotropes.**

A29.2 When a patient is admitted for treatment routinely requiring level 1 critical care this is noted and booked at the time of admission, ensuring that the required facilities and level of staff cover are available.

A29.3 The responsible consultant determines that level 1 critical care is required and personally hands over the patient to the responsible nurse.

A29.4 The patient is observed at regular intervals by nursing staff, the required level of observation is included in the patient's treatment plan and adjusted in response to recovery or deterioration of condition.

A29.5 While a patient is receiving level 1 critical care, the responsible consultant visits the patient a minimum of twice daily.

A29.6 If a patient deteriorates or otherwise fulfils the criteria for a higher level of critical care, admission to the hospital's critical care facility, or transfer to another critical care facility, is immediately effected.

A29.7 The responsible consultant determines that level 2 or 3 critical care is required and personally hands over the patient to the responsible nurse.

A29.8 Patients requiring level 2 or level 3 critical care receive this level of care either within the hospital or are transferred immediately to a facility that provides it.

A29.9 Where patients need level 2 or level 3 critical care after treatment as a matter of course, due to the seriousness of the operation type, the facilities for such care must be available within the hospital.

A29.10   Where level 2 or level 3 critical care is not provided within the hospital, contingency emergency transfer arrangements are in place that are documented and agreed in advance with each of the appropriate specialised units to which patients may be transferred.

A29.11   The transfer agreement includes the provision of a skilled retrieval team by the receiving unit.

A29.12   There are written criteria for the discharge of patients from critical care.

Level 2 or Level 3 Critical Care within the Hospital

OUTCOME

Patients are assured that where level 2 or level 3 critical care is provided, as appropriate, within the hospital, it is done so effectively.

STANDARD A30

A30.1   **Establishments with critical care facilities at level 2 or 3 have arrangements in place in line with the Intensive Care Society's *Standards for ICU* (1998) and the Department of Health's *Comprehensive Critical Care Report* (May 2000), including:**

- **written criteria for the admission of patients to critical care beds;**
- **a written policy and protocols for post-operative management;**
- **staff are briefed on the policy and protocols so that they are aware of what they should do in specific circumstances;**
- **pathology services, including a blood bank;**
- **critical care beds situated so that nursing staff are able to effectively observe the patient at all times;**
- **critical care beds have sufficient space on both sides to enable care to be delivered whilst all the necessary equipment is in place;**
- **arrangements for immediate back up and/or replacement in the event of equipment failure;**
- **records kept of the use of each ventilator (to enable appropriate servicing arrangements in line with the manufacturer's instructions).**

A30.2   Where critical care at level 2 or above is provided, staffing for critical care reflects the advice in the Department of Health *Comprehensive Critical Care Report* (May 2000), is based on patient dependency and ensures:

- a designated resident medical practitioner is on duty at all times, who has adult advanced life support certification;
- a registered nurse who has training in critical care nursing is on duty in charge of the unit at all times when there are patients in it;

- all clinical staff working in critical care have up to date training in critical care techniques, at least annually.

- a resuscitation team trained in advanced life support is on duty at all times;

- a radiographer with mobile imaging equipment is available on call;

- a physiotherapist experienced in critical care is available on call;

- where level 3 critical care is provided, the resident medical officer is experienced to specialist registrar standard in either anaesthetics or intensive care medicine.

A30.3 The responsible consultant and the anaesthetist visit the patient twice a day, as a minimum whilst they are receiving critical care at level 2 or 3.

Radiology

Published Guidance for the Conduct of Radiology

OUTCOME

Patients and staff are assured that ionising and non-ionising radiation are undertaken in a safe and protective environment.

STANDARD A31

A31.1 The provision and use of facilities using ionising radiation are undertaken in compliance with:

- **The Ionising Radiations Regulations 1999;**
- **The Approved Code of Practice and Guidance;**
- **The Ionising Radiation (Medical Exposure) Regulations 2000;**
- **associated professional guidance.**

A31.2 Those undertaking exposures utilising radiopharmaceuticals or sealed sources are informed by:

- The Ionising Radiations Regulations 1999;
- The Approved Code of Practice and Guidance;
- The Ionising Radiation (Medical Exposure) Regulations 2000;
- associated professional guidance.

A31.3 In addition they are informed by:

- The Medicines (Administration of Radioactive Substances) Amendment Regulations 1995;
- Notes for Guidance on the Clinical Administration of Radiopharmaceuticals and Use of Sealed Radioactive Sources.

A31.4 The provision and use of facilities using non-ionising radiation for medical exposures are undertaken in compliance with:

- Health Guidance Note – Magnetic Resonance Imaging (NHS Estates 1997);

- Health Building Note 6 Supplement 1 – Accommodation for Magnetic Resonance Imaging (NHS Estates 1994);

- Guidelines for Magnetic Resonance Diagnostic Equipment in Clinical Use (MDA 1993);

- MRI static magnetic field safety considerations (MDA DB 9803 1998);

- IPSM Report 70 Testing of Doppler Equipment;

- IPSM Report 71 Routine QA of Imaging Systems;

- Guidance Notes for Ultrasound Scanners used in the Examination of the Breast (MDA/98/52).

A31.5 There are written procedures for identifying patients with pacemakers and metallic implants.

A31.6 For MRI, special attention is given to the use of MRI compatible ancillary equipment.

A31.7 There are prominently displayed signs warning pregnant women of radiation dangers to the foetus (where appropriate to the patient profile of the hospital, these signs are multi-lingual),

Training and Qualifications of Staff Providing Radiology Services

OUTCOME

Radiological treatment is provided by appropriately trained and qualified health care professionals.

STANDARD A32

A32.1 In establishments where ionising radiation, radiopharmaceuticals or sealed sources are used a qualified and experienced person is appointed as a radiation protection adviser.

A32.2 The radiation protection adviser is involved with advising on compliance with statutory requirements and guidance, and where appropriate on the construction, design and layout of buildings where ionising radiations are or are about to be used.

A32.3 Those interpreting a wide range of diagnostic images are clinical radiologists on the GMC's specialist register.

A32.4   Where a wide range of examinations is provided, diagnostic examinations are performed by state registered diagnostic radiographers, trained sonographers and by medically qualified practitioners, trained in the examination techniques undertaken, in accordance with regulatory requirements.

A32.5   Diagnostic nuclear medicine examinations are carried out and reported only by qualified and experienced healthcare professionals.

A32.6   Those interpreting a wide range of nuclear medicine images are clinical radiologists or nuclear medicine physicians on the GMC's specialist register.

A32.7   Magnetic Resonance Imaging (MRI) and ultrasound examinations are carried out and reported only by qualified and experienced medical practitioners.

Pharmacy Services

Responsibility for Pharmaceutical Services

OUTCOME

Responsibility for obtaining, prescribing, storing, use, handling, recording and disposal of medicines is clear.

STANDARD A33

A33.1   The registered manager ensures that the safe and secure handling of medicines and medicines management is clearly defined.

A33.2   Hospitals have either:

- a pharmaceutical department; or

- alternative arrangements in place for comprehensive pharmaceutical services, including out of hours arrangements.

A33.3   Where a pharmaceutical department is provided it is under the control of a pharmacist who is a registered member of the Royal Pharmaceutical Society of Great Britain.

A33.4   The pharmacist is responsible for:

- the purchasing, quality, storage, dispensing and distribution of all medicines, as well as for ward based pharmaceutical services;

- advising on drug therapy, dosage, patient counselling and discharge medicine.

A33.5   Out of hours access to the pharmacy is restricted to the RMO and senior registered nurse on duty by a dual key system, which requires both key holders to be present in order to gain access.

Ordering, Storage, Use and Disposal of Medicines

OUTCOME

Medicines, dressings and gases are handled in a safe and secure manner.

STANDARD A34

A34.1   All medicines, medical gases and interactive wound dressings are obtained by, and stored under the control of a pharmacist, medical practitioner or registered nurse.

A34.2   The pharmacist or, where there is no pharmacist employed, the senior registered nurse, authorises any orders to obtain prescription-only medicines from wholesale suppliers.

A34.3   Labelling of medicines is clearly printed (or typed), not hand written. Stock items sent to wards have batch numbers and expiry dates.

A34.4   Medicines within a ward, theatre or department are the responsibility of the registered nurses designated for the purpose by the registered manager.

A34.5   A medication record is kept for each patient, the entries signed by the prescriber, showing:

- the name and date of birth of the patient;
- registration number and ward where appropriate;
- the name of the medicine;
- the dose;
- the route of administration;
- the frequency and time for administering each dose;
- the date of prescribing;
- any known hypersensitivity or allergies to medicines;
- any special requirements.

A34.6   Records are kept for eight years from the date of discharge or death of the patient.

A34.7   Medicines brought into the hospital by individual patients, and which are not used, are kept separate from other medicines on the ward and held in a safe place until discharge of the patient when they are returned to the patient or his/her representative if still clinically appropriate.

A34.8   There is a written policy on the use of patients' own medicines that facilitates an audit trail for the receipt, administration and return of medicines.

A34.9   The disposal of waste is carried out by an authorised contractor who is used to complying with the arrangements for pharmaceutical waste, including cytotoxic waste where appropriate.

A34.10   When a patient dies in the hospital, any medicines dispensed specifically for the patient are kept for at least one week in case there is a need for a coroner's inquest.

Administration of Medicines

OUTCOME

Prescription, supply and administration conform to the requirements of relevant legislation and best practice. Prescription, supply and administration of medicines is undertaken only by appropriately qualified, competent staff.

STANDARD A3

A35.1 **Medicines are administered by a medical practitioner or a registered nurse in accordance with the UKCC's *Guidelines for the administration of medicines* (October 2000), or by another health care professional assessed as competent to administer those medicines.**

A35.2 Specialist administration procedures are carried out by staff who have been assessed as competent in that area.

A35.3 The administration of controlled drugs is undertaken by a medical practitioner or registered nurse and is witnessed.

A35.4 There is a secure method for transporting medicines from the medicine cupboard to the patient.

A35.5 When medicines are no longer required by the named patient they are returned to the pharmacy.

Self-administration of Medicines

OUTCOME

Patients are assessed, consulted and advised before they are enabled to self-administer medicines.

STANDARD A36

A36.1 **There is a written policy and procedure for self-medication, which conforms to the duty of care inherent in the relationship of the hospital to the patient.**

A36.2 Where the risks have been assessed and it is deemed appropriate , patients are enabled to self-administer their medicines.

A36.3 Arrangements are made with the agreement of the patient, the registered nurse and the medical practitioner responsible for the patient's care.

A36.4 Medicines dispensed for patients to self-administer have full directions and BNF cautionary warning where appropriate.

A36.5   The medicine is stored in a personal lockable cupboard or drawer, the keys being held by the patient.

A36.6   There is a spare key to which clinical staff have access.

Medicines Management

> **OUTCOME**
>
> Measures are in place to ensure the safe and secure handling of medicines.

STANDARD A37

A37.1   The organisation reports adverse incidents involving medicinal products and devices to the relevant agency (the MCA, or the MDA), and appropriately manages any subsequent required action.

A37.2   There is a multi-professional, representative body, such as a Drug and Therapeutics Committee, that oversees the formulation, agreement and implementation of policies concerning medicines use.

Aseptic Dispensing, Non Sterile Manufacture and Repacking

> **OUTCOME**
>
> Aseptic dispensing is carried out safely and appropriately

STANDARD A38

A38.1   Arrangements for the provision of services such as parenteral nutrition, intravenous additives, and cytotoxics comply with the principles of EL(97)52 regarding unlicensed aseptic dispensing in hospital pharmacies.

A38.2   Non-sterile manufacturing, re-packing and extemporaneous preparation adhere to the principles outlined within the MCA's guide to good manufacturing practice.

Storage and Supply of Medical Gases

OUTCOME

Medical gases are stored and supplied appropriately.

STANDARD A39

A39.1 **There is a named Authorised Person MGPS (medical gas pipeline systems) responsible for the storage, identification, quality and purity of all gases at the terminal units, and for maintaining gas pipelines, and compliance with HTM 2022, this may be an appropriately qualified employee or through a contract with a medical gas company.**

A39.2 Where the Authorised Person is not employed on site at the hospital there is a named member of staff delegated to be his representative on the site as the Quality Controller of the medical gas pipeline system, who has training and familiarity with medical gas systems.

A39.3 Prior to use of a new system, or resumption of use of a repaired system, the named quality controller is required to indicate that he or she is satisfied with the operation of the pipelines system and the identity and purity of the gases at terminal units alongside the signature of the Authorised Person who accepts responsibility for the correct operation of the pipeline systems.

A39.4 Any engineers (competent persons) delegated to work on the medical gas pipelines systems have training and are authorised to do so by the Authorised Person.

A39. 5 All work on medical gas pipeline systems is controlled by a permit to work procedure, which includes ensuring that all paperwork with respect to work carried out on the medical gas pipeline system is copied to the Authorised Person.

A39.6 Policies and procedures are produced for recording the delivery, handling and storage of full and empty medical gas cylinders, with an indication of who is in charge of this procedure at each site.

Pathology Services

Management of Pathology Services

> **OUTCOME**
>
> Pathology services are provided by appropriately qualified and trained staff.

STANDARD A40

A40.1 **The provision of services is under the clinical supervision of a medically qualified pathologist or, in appropriate disciplines, a non-medical scientist of equivalent standing.**

A40.2 The head of the service is able to assume professional, scientific, consultative, organisational and administrative responsibilities for the service.

A40.3 It is the responsibility of the head of the service to ensure that the procedures and tests performed by technical staff are within the scope of their professional training and experience.

Pathology Services Process

> **OUTCOME**
>
> The process by which pathology services are undertaken provides quality assurance for patients.

STANDARD A41

A41.1 **Written policy and procedures describe the organisation and overall scope of the laboratory services, and describe:**

- **the provision of diagnostic and consultancy services to clinicians including the provision of reports;**
- **the scientific direction of the department including any research and development programmes;**
- **the maintenance of performance standards including quality control;**
- **safety aspects of the department;**
- **medical and technical responsibilities which are delegated to medical or other qualified laboratory personnel;**
- **the arrangements for the supply, storage, distribution and return of blood and blood components.**

A41.2   Written policies and procedures include arrangements for the integrated management of requests for collection of pathology specimens with documentation to ensure continuous identification of the individual from whom the specimen is collected.

A41.3   There are written policies and procedures for all arrangements for the transfer and transportation of specimens, which include:

- arrangements for the protection of those handling such items in transit;
- arrangements for the appropriate temperature-controlled storage of specimens.

A41.4   There are written policies and procedures for disposal of specimens and reagents used, including the disposal of clinical and other waste arising in the laboratory.

Quality Control of Pathology Services

OUTCOME

Quality control arrangements for pathology services provide quality assurance for patients.

STANDARD A42

A42.1   Written policies and procedures are in place for internal quality control and external quality assurance and indicate sources, dates of adoption and evidence of regular review.

A42.2   A written record of all reagents, calibration and quality control material is kept.

A42.3   The written policies and procedures include a description of the range of services provided and their method, for example in-house, by contract, out-of-hours.

A42.4   There are written procedures for the performance of each test, including preparation of equipment, samples and reagents, calculation of results and review of internal quality control and external quality assurance performance.

Facilities and Equipment for Pathology Services

OUTCOME

Pathology services are provided using safe and effective facilities and equipment.

STANDARD A43

A43.1 **Space is available for the collection of specimens, separate from the laboratory working areas.**

A43.2 There are designated storage areas for specimens, reagents and records.

A43.3 Where appropriate, mortuary and post-mortem facilities are available or formal contract arrangements are made for the provision of these, together with procedures for the identification and recording of patient identity and/or of specimen material.

Cancer Services

Chemotherapy

OUTCOME

Patients receive safe chemotherapy treatment.

STANDARD A44

A44.1 **There is a clinical director for the chemotherapy service who is a consultant medical oncologist, or a consultant haematologist, or other suitably qualified consultant.**

A44.2 Areas where chemotherapy is administered have equipment readily available for the management of emergencies including anaphylaxis, extravasation, cardiac arrest and spillage of cytotoxics.

A44.3 Registered nurses administering chemotherapy have undertaken the N59 course, or equivalent and their competence has been assessed.

A44.4 Where children are treated by chemotherapy, nurses have undertaken the ENB course for children's chemotherapy.

A44.5 There are documented standard chemotherapy regimes and procedures for handling situations outside the standard regimes.

A44.6 There are written procedures/protocols for the prevention and treatment of complications arising from chemotherapy.

A44.7   There is written information for patients undergoing chemotherapy, which includes advice and action to be taken if the patient develops side effects or complications.

A44.8   The information for patients is available prior to starting chemotherapy.

A44.9   The responsibilities of the pharmaceutical service are documented in relation to chemotherapy.

A44.10   All cytotoxic chemotherapy prescriptions are checked and signed by a pharmacist.

A44.11   Chemotherapy treatment records are kept which include:

- treatment intention;
- route of administration;
- number of cycles intended;
- frequency of cycles and of administrations within a cycle;
- toxicities which require a dose modification;
- whether the course was completed or not.

Radiotherapy

OUTCOME

Patients receive safe radiotherapy services.

STANDARD A45

A45.1   Radiotherapy services are provided under the clinical direction of a consultant clinical oncologist.

A45.2   The following equipment is available for the delivery of radiotherapy services:

- two linear accelerators, or one with backup arrangements;
- treatment planning computer with 3D planning facility;
- simulator;
- superficial x-ray and electron therapy facilities;
- mould room;
- facilities for the use of unsealed isotopes, where appropriate.

A45.3   Radiotherapy physicists are directly employed or work sessionally under contract and the staffing levels for the volume comply with the recommendations of the Institute of Physics and Engineering in Medicine.

A45.4   All requests for a course of radiotherapy are documented and are classified as urgent, palliative or radical.

A45.5   There is written information for patients undergoing radiotherapy, which includes advice and action to be taken if the patient develops side effects or complications.

A45.6   The information for patients is made available prior to commencing the radiotherapy treatment.

A45.7   Records are kept of all radiotherapy given and these are stored within, or immediately accessible to the service at all times.

A45.8   The records include as a minimum:

- radiographs or other treatment planning images;
- treatment plans and dose calculation sheets.

A45.9   There is access to CT scanner facilities for planning radical treatments.

A45.10   There are written procedures, which set out maximum and minimum doses and how the dose for each treatment is calculated.

A45.11   All patient-related treatment information and individualised immobilisation aids include the patient's name and unique identification number.

A45.12   There is a written procedure to ensure correct identification of the patient before each treatment starts.

A45.13   There is a quality management system in place, which includes radiation therapy equipment quality control.

10 Mental Health Establishments

Introduction to Standards M1 to M47

The standards for mental health establishments apply to those non-NHS establishments which, for the purposes of section 2(3) of the Care Standards Act 2000, come under the definition of 'independent hospital' because either:

- the main purpose of the establishment is to provide medical or psychiatric treatment for mental disorder and it has at least one overnight bed; and/or

- treatment or nursing (or both) are provided in the establishment for persons liable to be detained under the Mental Health Act 1983.

These standards apply, therefore, to a range of premises where mental health treatment is provided, including the large mental health hospitals, smaller establishments that provide mental health treatment as their main or sole purpose, and all establishments that take people who are liable to be detained.

With the exception of standard M1 (Working with the Mental Health National Service Framework), the standards for adult mental health establishments are applicable to establishments providing mental health services for children and adolescents (a Children's National Service Framework has been announced, with child and adolescent mental health services (CAMHS) to be a component).

The standards fall into two categories:

- they begin with those that apply to all mental health establishments (including for children and adolescents) that come within the definition of 'independent hospital' (as set out above);

- they end with those that, in addition, apply to mental health establishments that can take people liable to be detained (including children and adolescents).

These standards do not apply to care homes, nor to establishments that mainly provide counselling or to psychiatrists' consulting rooms.

In formulating these standards key stakeholders within the NHS, Local Authorities and the independent sector were engaged in discussion and a search of the literature was conducted. In addition, 43 reports from inquiries into mental health services published between 1990 and 2000 were studied and the main recommendations subjected to a thematic analysis and re-written as standards. These inquiries demonstrated the tragic consequences which can follow if specific fundamental practices are not inherent within services and provided a salutary reminder of the need to have robust management systems in place if these errors are not to be repeated.

[See: Department of Health *Mental Health National Service Frameworks* (1999); Health Advisory Service 2000 Standards for *Adult Mental Health Services* (1999).]

Quality of Treatment and Care (standards M1 to M4)

These standards concern the overall management of the mental health services provided by the regulated establishment, including the need for it to reflect the Mental Health National Service Framework. They recognise that services, whatever sector they operate in, do not work in isolation and require mechanisms to link with and be influenced by external agencies operating at a national, regional and local level.

Human Resources (standards M5 to M6)

These standards recognise the importance of services having the right numbers, type and skill-mix of appropriately trained staff. References made in these mental health standards to 'clinical staff' and 'clinicians' cover both health care and social care professionals to reflect their involvement in the delivery of mental health services.

Risk Management (standards M7 to M10)

Risk management aims to achieve the optimum balance between good quality care, treatment and rehabilitation of patients. This will be achieved through an ongoing process of identifying and assessing risks, with the objective of improved prevention, control and containment of risks.

The management of such risks is a key organisational responsibility. All managers and clinicians must accept the management of risks as one of their fundamental duties, and every member of staff must have a real sense of ownership and commitment to identifying and minimising risks.

Patient Treatment and Care (standards M11 to M35)

The Care Programme Approach (CPA) was introduced in 1991 (Department of Health Circular HC(90)23) to provide a framework for caring for people with mental health problems. The four major components are:

- assessment of health and social care needs and any risks involved;
- nomination of a care co-ordinator;
- preparation of a care plan;
- regular review of the care plan.

The CPA is aimed at providing a comprehensive service that addresses health and social care needs and gives priority within the service to those people with substantial and complex needs arising from mental disorder. It aims to focus sensitively on the particular needs of individual patients and their carers by supporting people in their own communities where possible, and recognising their complex individual networks of care which encompass all areas of their life.

The CPA is applicable to all adults of working age in contact with the secondary mental health system (health and social care), though not a requirement. The principles of the CPA are also relevant to the care and treatment of younger and older people with mental health problems.

Essential elements are the maximising of service users' and carers' participation in the planning and provision of care and the improvement of co-ordination and avoidance of duplication between services. The continuity of care is enhanced by the use of care co-ordinators supported by effective multi-disciplinary teams.

Empowerment: the involvement of patients in their individualised care, as well as in planning and implementation of services is seen as an essential component of contemporary mental health care. Without a successful range of methods to engage patients and their representative bodies, mental health services would be seen as failing to operate a service which reflected client needs or was truly inclusive. There are no quick fix solutions. It is a lengthy process of attitude and cultural change requiring personal reflection and a desire to reverse the balance of power.

Anti-discriminatory Practice: it is essential that independent health care providers adopt a strong value base in applying principles of anti-discriminatory practice in their approach to patient care. Services must be proactive in addressing the needs of individual patients with due regard to race, ethnicity, religion, gender, age and sexuality and so forth.

Least-restrictive Environment: the principle of people having timely access to an appropriate hospital bed in the least restrictive environment, consistent with the need to protect them and the public, has been government policy for some years. This has been reiterated as part of the Mental Health National Service Framework.

The concept of 'least restrictive' is not just the level of security but the mode of operation of the facility. Some residential units in secure hospitals operate a less restrictive regime than that which might be operated in a medium and even low secure unit when measured in terms of: access to own room, numbers of possessions, access to grounds, on and off residential unit visiting etc. In promoting the principle of least restrictive environment the challenge is for services to move away from blanket policies and procedures to the justification of restrictions for individual patients on the basis of demonstrable risk.

Additional Standards for Child and Adolescent Mental Health Services (standards M36 to M40)

These standards aim to ensure that the special needs of children and adolescents receiving mental health treatment are properly addressed. They supplement the child protection requirements in the core standards.

Establishments for Patients Detained under the Mental Health Act 1983 (standards M41 to M47)

The Mental Health Act 1983 provides the legal framework for the reception, care, treatment and discharge of mentally disordered patients, the management of their property and other related matters. It sets out the legal requirements necessary to receive people suffering from a mental disorder into hospital care for assessment and/or treatment and the systems of appeal and review open to the individual.

The Act specifies particular safeguards with respect to consent to treatment and establishes an independent body, the Mental Health Act Commission (MHAC), whose role is to protect the rights of individuals held under the Mental Health Act and to try to ensure the correct application of procedures. This is achieved through a rolling programme of visits by the MHAC to all facilities that detain patients under the Act.

The Code of Practice of the Mental Health Act 1983 provides guidance on how staff should proceed when undertaking duties under the Act and covers specific guidance on: assessment prior to possible admission under the Mental Health Act, admission under the Mental Health Act to hospital and guardianship, treatment and care in hospital, leaving hospital, and handling particular groups of patients. The Act does not impose a legal duty to comply with the Code but as it is a statutory document, failure to follow it could be referred to in evidence in legal proceedings.

In addition, the Code of Practice makes a number of recommendations about other matters which hospital managers should address, including:

- ensuring that the grounds for admitting the patient are valid and reasonable, and that all detention documents are in order;
- exercising the power to transfer under the Act certain categories of detained patients to another hospital administered by the same authority, to a Special Health Authority or to a hospital in another district;
- ensuring that those formally delegated to receive documents and all those who will be required to scrutinise admission documents have a thorough knowledge of the Act;
- giving information to patients and their relatives;
- ensuring that any patient who wishes to apply to a Mental Health Review Tribunal is provided with assistance to progress and given all the necessary information;
- reviewing patients' detention.

See also, in particular, regulations 43 to 47 of the Private and Voluntary Health Care Regulations.

Quality of Treatment and Care

Working with the Mental Health National Service Framework (applies to adult mental health establishments only)

OUTCOME

Patients receive treatment and care that reflects the Mental Health National Service Framework.

STANDARD M1

M1.1 **There is a written policy and supporting procedures that reflect the Mental Health National Service Framework.**

M1.2 The policy demonstrates the working links and liaison channels between the establishment and NHS Trusts, Health Authorities and other commissioners of mental health services, social services, housing, primary health care, the criminal justice system and other independent organisations.

M1.3 The registered manager ensures that the establishment contributes to the work of the Mental Health National Service Framework. If appropriate, this may involve membership of the local implementation team.

Communication Between Staff

OUTCOME

Patient treatment and care is informed by clear communication between staff.

STANDARD M2

M2.1 **There are written policies and procedures to ensure effective communication between staff in relation to the treatment of a patient.**

M2.2 Information is shared between all staff involved in the provision of a patient's health and social care including the sharing of information at any handovers.

M2.3 The policy includes procedures for conducting nursing handovers between shifts.

M2.4 All involved with the patient's care are aware of any relevant long-term history.

M2.5   There is accurate and timely documentation in the patient's health records (care plan) of all interventions by staff, with each entry signed and dated by the health care professional on a daily basis. Where care assistants make entries these are countersigned and evaluated by a health professional.

M2.6   When there is a change of responsible medical practitioner a full clinical hand-over takes place, including transfer of records.

Patient Confidentiality

> **OUTCOME**
>
> Patients are assured of confidentiality.

STANDARD M3

M3.1   There are written policies and procedures for maintaining the confidentiality of all details in relation to a patient's treatment and balancing this against any risk to the patient, staff or members of the public.

M3.2   Managers ensure that staff have access to guidance and training so that they understand when it is important to share information about patient needs and difficulties, balancing the requirements of confidentiality and risk management.

M3.3   Staff are aware of the over-riding duty to breach confidentiality where there is a potential risk to the patient, staff or members of the public.

M3.4   The limits of confidentiality between the various professionals concerned with a patient's care are carefully defined, indicating the circumstances in which others must be informed.

Clinical Audit

> **OUTCOME**
>
> Patients' treatment and care is assured by clinical audit.

STANDARD M4

M4.1   Clinical audit programmes are undertaken that include:

- **monitoring of multi-professional working in mental health care teams;**
- **monitoring multi-professional contributions to health records;**
- **the extent and quality of direct staff-patient contact.**

M4.2   Clinical standards performance and serious/untoward incidents are audited at least annually.

M4.3   The auditing of serious/untoward incidents is led by a senior clinician and a full multi-disciplinary team.

M4.4   Audits of clinical performance (including the administration of medication) will have an identified lead senior clinician who ensures that the standards being audited are consistent with professional good practice and makes recommendations on changes to practise as required

M4.5   The quality of implementation of the Care Programme Approach is audited, to ensure consistent and appropriate application, including:

- the quality of care plans;

- the attainment of treatment goals;

- particularly for those with multiple needs, the effectiveness of inter-agency working.

M4.6   The views of patients and their carers are routinely sought and are used as an indicator of the quality of services and included in any audit of service delivery.

M4.7   A record is maintained (and used in audits of service delivery) of:

- emergency re-admissions;

- the number of patients applying for managers' review of detention and the outcomes of such applications;

- the number of patients applying for review by Mental Health Review Tribunals (distinguishing between patients' applications and those made when patients have not exercised this right) and the outcomes of such applications.

Human Resources

Staff Numbers and Skill Mix

OUTCOME

The numbers, type and skills of clinicians ensure that patients are appropriately treated and cared for at all times.

STANDARD M5

M5.1   The numbers and skills of clinicians and support staff assigned to each unit reflect the number and needs of patients on each unit.

M5.2   There is a named nurse/care co-ordinator and associate nurse/carer system to ensure continuity of care across all shifts.

M5.3   Nursing/care co-ordinators are appointed only from amongst staff who are on duty for a significant part of a patient's stay in hospital.

M5.4   The roles and responsibilities of each member of the multi-professional team are documented and staff members are aware of their own responsibilities and the roles and responsibilities of the other team members.

Staff Training

OUTCOME

Patients receive treatment and care from appropriately trained staff.

STANDARD M6

M6.1   All clinical staff receive training on the values, principles and broad standards of the National Service Framework and information about how this impacts upon their own work (e.g. the local implementation of the Mental Health Service Framework)

M6.2   Joint programmes of staff training are made available to optimise the working of the multi-professional teams and to establish a mutual understanding of issues and each others roles.

M6.3   All staff receive training in risk assessment, and understand when to refer patients for expert guidance in the context of multi-professional working. This training is tailored to individual practitioner needs, with refresher courses as appropriate.

M6.4   All clinical staff receive training which is updated at least annually, in how to manage individuals who may be disturbed, aggressive, troubled, suicidal or distressed.

M6.5   Clinical staff receive training, including annual up-dating, on the prevention management of aggression and techniques to defuse situations and in physical intervention techniques according to current guidelines.

M6.6   The use of clinical policies and guideline documents are included in training programmes.

M6.7   Clinical staff are trained in resuscitation procedures.

M6.8   Training and education programmes include training in anti-discriminatory practice.

M6.9   Clinical staff are trained to meet the needs of disabled people including understanding the complexities of those with sensory impairment.

M6.10   Staff induction and ongoing training makes reference to professional regulation and accountability.

Risk Management

Risk Assessment and Management

OUTCOME

All potential environmental and clinical risks are assessed and managed to ensure a safe environment is maintained for patients, staff and the general public.

STANDARD M7

M7.1 **There is a written risk management policy, which:**

- **takes account of who might be harmed and how;**
- **requires that the precise nature of the risks are recorded in writing;**
- **requires action to be taken in response to the risks identified and is documented;**
- **outlines a regular review system for levels of risk to be revised in the light of new information.**

M7.2 An annual audit is undertaken by a senior clinician (experienced in managing challenging behaviour) and the Health and Safety Officer to review the safety, security and appropriateness of the facilities for the client group. Actions are identified and responses recorded.

M7.3 Individual clinical risk assessments are undertaken by the multidisciplinary team at least every 3 months and following a serious/untoward incident or adverse health event or near miss involving the patient.

M7.4 The patient is involved in his or her own risk assessment and the patient's views are included in the written record of the risk assessment.

M7.5 All individuals working for the service, including students and those in a voluntary capacity, are alerted to the potential risks of violence or self-harm by the patient, and have ready access to professional support.

Suicide Prevention

> **OUTCOME**
>
> Patients are protected from self-harm, including risk of suicide.

STANDARD M8

M8.1 **There are written polices, protocols and procedures on the prevention of homicides and suicide, which take account of the recommendations of the confidential inquiry into homicide and suicides (Department of Health's *Safer Services* (1999) and *Safety First* (2001)).**

M8.2 Where an assessment of an individual's risk of self-harm or suicide indicates the need for special precautions, details of all interventions are recorded in the care plan including:

- the appropriate level of observation and engagement to be used; and

- the recording of such observations.

M8.3 Any factors that suggest that a patient has been or might be a suicide risk (including any diagnosis of severe mental illness, previous attempts of self-harm, statements of intent, family history of suicide, or detentions under the Mental Health Act) are recorded in case summaries and discharge letters.

M8.4 All clinicians and support staff are made aware of the risks to patients associated with periods of change and significant dates, and increase vigilance at these times.

M8.5 Arrangements are in place to regularly review the physical environment and steps are taken to reduce access to means of suicide, including the use of window restrictors.

M8.6 Local suicide/self-harm audits are undertaken to learn the lessons.

Infection Control

> **OUTCOME**
>
> The risk of patients, staff and visitors acquiring a health care associated infection is minimised.

STANDARD M9

M9.1 **Infection control advice is available, particularly in relation to the following:**

- **the development of policies relating to engineering and building services for the hospital and to the purchase of medical devices/equipment, including early stage planning;**

- **all stages of the contracting process for services, which have implications for infection control, for example, housekeeping, laundry, clinical waste.**

M9.2 Written policies, procedures and guidance for the prevention and control of infection are implemented and reflect relevant legislation and published professional guidance, including:

- major outbreaks of communicable infections;

- isolation of patients; and

- control of tuberculosis, including multi-drug resistant tuberculosis.

Resuscitation Procedures

OUTCOME

Patients are resuscitated appropriately and effectively.

STANDARD M10

M10.1 **There are written resuscitation policies and procedures in place, which include guidance on when to summon an ambulance.**

M10.2 Prominently labelled and easily accessible resuscitation equipment is checked and restocked weekly and a record kept, which includes a list of the equipment.

M10.3 There is a member of staff on duty at all times who is trained (and updated at least annually) in first-aid and resuscitation techniques.

Patient Treatment and Care

The Care Programme Approach/Care Management

OUTCOME

Patients receive treatment and care in line with the Care Programme Approach/Care Management.

STANDARD M11

M11.1 **There are written policies and procedures, reviewed at least every three years, that implement the requirements of the Care Programme Approach (CPA)/Care Management in accordance with Health Service Guidelines.**

M11.2 There is a tiered approach to the implementation of the CPA/Care Management.

M11.3 There is a tier for patients receiving care from a single health care worker or qualified social worker (simple CPA/Care Management). These patients have an agreed care plan without involving large amounts of paperwork.

M11.4 There is a tier for those receiving complex, multi-disciplinary care with requirements for regular review (enhanced CPA/Care Management). These patients have a formally allocated care co-ordinator, who is not generally the responsible consultant.

Admission and Assessment

OUTCOME

Patients are admitted and assessed appropriately.

STANDARD M12

M12.1 There are written policies and procedures for voluntary admission, agreed between the relevant agencies.

M12.2 Patients receive a comprehensive assessment (including a physical health assessment) on admission or transfer from another team.

M12.3 When a patient is referred for the first time, or transferred from another team, a new clinical assessment is carried out and includes an assessment of risk of harm to self or others by the patient.

M12.4 The assessment process includes an assessment of the family employment and social circumstances of patients, and for children their educational needs, especially those with behavioural problems after admission and prior to discharge.

M12.5 All assessments include the patient's known substance misuse including alcohol history with intake expressed in units of alcohol.

M12.6 There is a system to ensure the early identification of the patient's needs and strengths as an individual, as well as in terms of his or her illness.

M 12.7 The assessment is clearly linked to the CPA/Care Management plan to ensure a follow-through is achieved

CPA Care Planning and Review

OUTCOME

Each patient has a care plan that addresses their needs appropriately.

STANDARD M13

M13.1 There is a single detailed, multi-professional plan of care formulated for each individual patient.

M13.2 The multi-professional care plan is prepared under the direction of the responsible consultant psychiatrist and/or care co-ordinator.

M13.3 Those who are responsible for the aftercare of the patient contribute towards the plan.

M13.4 The plan provides for both the long-term and immediate needs of the patient.

M13.5 The care plan for inpatients includes a specific programme of therapeutic activities within the clinical area that is relevant to the patient's needs which addresses employment, education and leisure, and assists rehabilitation.

M13.6 The care plan recognises and reflects diversity through attention to the patient's culture, ethnicity, gender, age and sexuality.

M13.7 A copy of the plan is given to the patient (who should sign it if possible) and to all those involved in his/her care.

M13.8 The care plan is subject to regular multi-professional reviews led by the care co-ordinator.

M13.9 At each review meeting the date of the next review is set and recorded.

Information for Patients on their Treatment

OUTCOME

Patients are effectively involved in decisions about their treatment.

STANDARD M14

M14.1 The patient is informed of the effect of the treatment being proposed, and his/her views are taken into account.

M14.2 The patient's ability to consent to treatment is assessed and the extent to which a patient's agreement to medication is given readily or with reservation is recorded.

M14.3 The medication regime of each patient, and the known side effects and risks, is explained fully to the patient and their carers. This information includes a publication date and is updated in response to changes in medication used and published research findings.

M14.4 Each patient receives the lowest dosage and number of medications necessary.

M14.5 Individual patients' views about their care plan and treatment, especially about the effects and side effects of drugs, are documented in the patient's health record (care plan), together with the response of the clinicians.

Patients with Developmental Disabilities

OUTCOME

The rights and needs of patients with developmental disabilities are recognised and addressed.

STANDARD M15

M15.1 There are written policies and procedures for ensuring that the rights and needs of patients with developmental disabilities are recognised and addressed. These are in line with current best practice (including Learning Disability Strategy 2001).

M15.2 An assessment of the patient's abilities including their ability to give informed consent is recorded in their health record.

M15.3 There is evidence (recorded in the patient's health record) that the patient is encouraged to participate in all decisions related to their care.

M15.4 Information is provided in a format designed to aid comprehension (e.g. use of Makaton).

M15.5 A multidisciplinary assessment and care plan to meet the patient's social needs (which includes the patent's views) is recorded in the patient's health record. This assessment and plan includes contact with family/significant others and the patient's expressed sexual needs.

M15.6 Within the clinical team there is evidence of training and expertise in caring for patients with developmental disabilities, so that the necessary knowledge base and skills are available to develop and maximise each patient's potential.

M15.7 All patients have received a general health check (with specific reference to sight, hearing and dental care) at least once within the last year.

M15.8 There are specialist teachers to provide tuition for adolescent patients with sight and hearing impairments.

Electro-convulsive Therapy (ECT)

OUTCOME

ECT is provided to patients safely and appropriately.

STANDARD M16

M16.1 There are written policies and procedures, reviewed at least every three years, on the use of electro-convulsive therapy (ECT).

M16.2 The facilities, equipment and operation of ECT meet the recommendations made in the ECT handbook (Royal College of Psychiatrists 1995).

M16.3 There is regular audit to ensure that ECT is carried out in line with the policies and procedures for its use and administration.

Administration of Medicines

OUTCOME

Appropriately trained and qualified clinicians administer all medicines to patients.

STANDARD M17

M17.1 There is a policy to include consent to treatment and administration to patients sectioned under the Mental Health Act. A copy of the current Certificate of Consent to Treatment (Form 38) or Certificate of Second Opinion (Form 39) – and if relevant s.61 Review of Treatment/MHAC 1 – is attached to the patients medicine card and checked by a registered nurse each time the relevant medication is administered. The written policy on consent to treatment includes clear guidance on:

- **treatment under s.57 requiring consent and a second opinion, ie psychosurgery,**
- **implantation of hormones;**
- **treatment under s.58 requiring consent or a second opinion, ie electro-convulsive therapy (ECT) and medication;**
- **nurses and the administration of medication**
- **withdrawal of consent**
- **second opinion appointed doctors (SOAD)**
- **review of Treatment under s.61 – including provision of a copy of the MHAC1 for the patient**
- **urgent treatment under s.62**

M17.2 All Certificates of Consent to Treatment (Form 38) and Certificates of Second Opinion (Form 39) are audited on a regular basis.

M17.3 All medicine is administered to a patient with a written prescription or, internal to the establishment, a drug administration chart that has been authorised by a legally authorised prescriber taking the provisions of Part IV of the Mental Health Act 1983 into account where appropriate.

M17.4 A medication record is kept for each patient, the entries signed by the prescriber, showing:

- the name and date of birth of the patient;
- registration number and ward where appropriate;
- the name of the medicine;
- the dose; and
- the date of prescribing.

M17.5 There are clear policies for the administration of 'when required' medicines.

M17.6 Where necessary, arrangements are in place for providing a second consultee (i.e. neither a medical practitioner nor a nurse) for visits of second opinion appointed medical practitioner.

M17.7 When medicines are no longer required by the named patient they are returned to the pharmacy or pharmacist for disposal.

Self-administration of Medicines

OUTCOME

Patients are assessed, consulted and advised before they are enabled to self-administer medicines.

STANDARD M18

M18.1 There is a written policy and procedure for self-medication, which conforms to the duty of care inherent in the relationship of the hospital to the patient.

M18.2 Where the risks have been assessed and it is deemed that they are at a minimal risk of endangering themselves or others, patients are enabled to self-administer their medicines.

M18.3 Arrangements are only made with the agreement of the registered nurse, the patient and the medical practitioner responsible for the patient's care.

M18.4 Medicines dispensed for patients to self-administer have full directions and BNF cautionary warning where appropriate.

M18.5 Regular checks are made on the quantity of medicine given to the patient to ensure the patient is taking the medication as prescribed.

M18.6　The medicine is stored in a personal lockable cupboard or drawer, the keys being held by the patient.

M18.7　There is a spare key to which clinical staff have access.

Treatment for Addictions

OUTCOME

Patients with addictions receive appropriate treatment and care.

STANDARD M19

M19.1　There are written policies and procedures, reviewed at least every three years, for the management of patients who may be abusing alcohol or drugs.

M19.2　Treatment sessions are in accordance with written guidance as part of the clinical programme and include:

- individual counselling;
- group therapy;
- community group meetings; and
- education sessions.

M19.3　There are written policies and procedures, which are reviewed at least every three years, for alcohol and drug testing during treatment which details the possible consequences of a positive test result.

Transfer of Patients

OUTCOME

The transfer of patients takes place safely and effectively.

STANDARD M20

M20.1　There are written policies and procedures to ensure the safe transfer of patients.

M20.2　There is full multi-professional exchange of information and discussion when patients are transferred from one residential unit or service to another.

M20.3　There are clearly identified plans and protocols in place for meeting the needs of people moving from one service to another.

M20.4　There are standards and targets for facilitating internal transfers to and from critical care facilities where provided.

Patient Discharge

OUTCOME

The discharge of patients takes place appropriately and effectively.

STANDARD M21

M21.1 There are written policies and procedures, reviewed at least every three years, about patient discharge.

M21.2 The policies and procedures cover arrangements to ensure that:

- discharge planning takes place as soon as possible after admission;
- patients and carers are involved in discharge planning;
- patients are provided with a copy of their care plan;
- multi-professional post-discharge plans are devised;
- GP and primary care teams are informed;
- the police are informed of the discharge of any patient with a history of sex offending.

M21.3 Discharge is a systematic and planned event.

M21.4 A co-ordination meeting is held prior to discharge to assess needs and nominate a care co-ordinator, where various sources of social work assistance are provided to discharged patients.

M21.5 Aftercare planning addresses the needs of the patient's carers as part of the implementation of the Carers (Recognition and Services) Act 1995.

M21.6 A crisis or contingency plan is agreed.

M21.7 Decisions to discharge or transfer patients are based on an assessment of the circumstances leading to hospitalisation as well as assessment of changes in other aspects of behaviour.

M21.8 Discharge planning meetings held under the auspices of the CPA are attended by all personnel, disciplines and agencies relevant to the care of the patient.

M21.9 Any referral to another agency (including a voluntary agency) for a specific service is confirmed in writing and a copy of the care plan is made available.

M21.10 Every attempt is made to ensure that, when a patient leaves hospital under the CPA, the care co-ordinator enables the patient to register with a GP.

M21.11 A discharge summary is sent to the patient's GP within one week of discharge which contain details of:

- diagnosis;
- treatment;

- follow-up arrangements;
- prognosis;
- a concise explanation of the condition;
- an accurate record of any violent incident;
- aspects of social care.

M21.12 An assessment of the risk of danger and self-harm is included in the discharge summary.

Patients' Records

OUTCOME

Patients' treatment and care is informed by accurate and comprehensive records.

STANDARD M22

M22.1 Professional notes are integrated into a single, multi-disciplinary record, which includes hospital and community records.

M22.2 The multi-disciplinary record is chronologically ordered to reflect the care given to the patient over time.

Empowerment

OUTCOME

Patients are informed about their rights, their treatment and how to obtain independent advocacy.

STANDARD M23

M23.1 Patient information leaflets (in the language(s) of the patients being cared for) are published and disseminated to patients, their family and carers about:

- **patients rights;**
- **responsibilities;**
- **medication;**
- **therapies.**

M23.2 All new patients are given written details of local organisations providing independent advocacy.

M23.3 Details of local organisations providing independent advocacy are displayed in the establishment.

Arrangements for Visiting

OUTCOME

Appropriate visiting arrangements are in place, about which patients and their visitors are clear.

STANDARD M24

M24.1 There is a written policy and information on arrangements for patients to have visits from family, friends and their carers.

M24.2 The policy and the information for patients and visitors includes:

- the circumstances when visiting may properly be restricted;

- what may not be brought into the establishment; and

- makes specific reference to the access and supervision of children.

M24.3 The policy on visiting is explained to all patients and visitors.

M24.4 Visiting normally takes place outside the times set aside for structured activities.

M24.5 Staff provide assistance to patients who need help to resist unwanted visiting, and assistance to visitors to resist unreasonable demands for visiting.

M24.6 If staff believe that visiting is disruptive to a patient's treatment programme they take responsibility for discussing this with visitors and patients.

Working with Carers and Family Members

OUTCOME

Staff involve patients' carers and families, as appropriate, in aspects of the treatment and care provided.

STANDARD M25

M25.1 There are written policies and procedures, reviewed at least every three years, about arrangements to involve the patient's family members, friends and carers.

M25.2 The policy includes principles and practices governing:

- relationships between staff and the patient's family, friends and carers;

- family members', friends' and carers' rights to information; and

- practical assistance and emotional support to be given to family, friends and carers.

M25.3 There are written policies and procedures for involving, with the patient's consent, families, carers and people close to the patient in:

- taking social and family histories into account following admission;
- drawing up, agreeing and reviewing treatment and care plans;
- planning and delivering services, particularly around discharge and after-care.

M25.4 Staff, patients, carers and families are fully informed of these procedures.

M25.5 Carers and family members are informed of opportunities to make appointments to see the care co-ordinator, responsible medical officer, consultant or other staff within a reasonable time.

M25.6 Clinical staff are encouraged to see the families and carers of patients and take account of their insights and knowledge and, where appropriate, record relevant information provided by family members and/or carers in the patient's file.

Anti-discriminatory Practice

OUTCOME

Patients are not discriminated against.

STANDARD M26

M26.1 There is a flexible and responsive regime which enables patients to be different from each other, meet their personal, health care, religious, cultural and language needs and which does not restrict their personal rights.

M26.2 The service has a written statement on patients' rights displayed in a public area and given to patients on admission.

M26.3 This statement includes the patient's rights to:
- be given comprehensive information about the nature of care services available;
- be treated with privacy and dignity;
- receive impartial access to all treatment services without discrimination;
- confidentiality about treatment and records;
- be free from mental, physical and chemical abuse and mechanical restraint;
- have complaints investigated;
- refuse treatment in certain circumstances;
- have access to translation and/or translation services.

Quality of Life for Patients

> **OUTCOME**
>
> The care provided recognises patients' personal needs.

STANDARD M27

M27.1 Separate areas are provided for patients requiring different levels and types of nursing care, such as:

- patients on acute admission residential units;
- patients who are likely to present severe behavioural problems;
- frail elderly mentally infirm patients;
- mothers suffering from post-natal depression accompanied by their babies;
- young people; or
- vulnerable patients likely to be exploited.

M27.2 Patients are accommodated in a single bedroom unless the care plan indicates otherwise and/or the patient has made a choice to share a room. (For children see standard M37.2).

M27.3 In forensic services and locked residential units there are gender specific facilities to meet the needs of patients with severe emotional and behavioural disorders.

M27.4 Safe facilities are provided for patients which safeguard their privacy and dignity including fully segregated dressing, washing and toilet facilities for men and women.

M27.5 Within reasonable limits patients have freedom of choice, have privacy, are allowed to participate in activities, and have a quality of life consistent with their individual care plan and the interests of other patients. In particular patients are allowed:

- choice of bedtime and rising (for children this will be personal to their age and needs);
- to dress as one chooses;
- access to drinks and food outside of set meal times;
- choice of foods at meal times;
- payment for work;
- access to library, music, art, current affairs etc;
- personal belongings consistent with the space available, including plants;
- privacy in relationships;
- to maintain outside links through trips and visits.

Patients' Money

OUTCOME

Patients' financial interests are safeguarded.

STANDARD M28

M28.1 The registered manager ensures that patients control their own money, except where they state that they do not wish to or they lack capacity, and that safeguards are in place to protect the interests of the patient.

M28.2 Written records of all transactions are maintained.

M28.3 Where the money of individual patients is handled, the manager ensures that the personal allowances of these patients are not pooled and that appropriate records and receipts are kept.

M28.4 The registered manager may be appointed as agent for a patient only where no other individual is available. In this case, the manager ensures that:

- the National Care Standards Commission is notified on inspection;
- records are kept of all incoming and outgoing payments.

M28.5 If the manager is to be an appointee for social security purposes, the Benefits Agency/Job Centre Plus is given appropriate notice.

M28.6 Using a risk assessment basis, those patients deemed capable have a facility to hold their own money. Secure facilities are also provided for the safe-keeping of money and valuables on behalf of patients.

Restrictions and Security for Patients

OUTCOME

Arrangements for the restriction and security of patients are clear and effective.

STANDARD M29

M29.1 There are policies and procedures that state whether each unit is to be locked or whether patients have free access in and out of the unit.

M29.2 On each occasion a residential unit which is normally open is locked, it is reported to the most senior service manager with a brief explanation of why it was locked.

Levels of Observation

> **OUTCOME**
>
> Appropriate arrangements are made for the observation of patients.

STANDARD M30

M30.1 **There are written policies and procedures, which are reviewed at least every three years, for determining levels of observation, engagement, communication and supervision for inpatients.**

M30.2 The policies are in line with guidance from the SNMAC (Standing Nursing and Midwifery Advisory Council).

M30.3 The policies state the:

- defined levels of observation determined by the senior medical practitioner on the residential unit, or in his/her absence, the senior registered nurse;
- the specified levels of observation including intervals of observation;
- details of numbers and skill levels of staff and their proximity to the patient under observation;
- criteria for each level of observation;
- criteria for reviewing patients levels of observation;
- length of time staff spent on observation.

M30.4 The policies ensure that all patients on a residential unit are considered subject to general observation, which includes actively engaging and interacting with the patient.

M30.5 Clinical staff are aware of, and consistently implement, clinical policies in relation to supportive observation and engagement.

M30.6 The reasons for imposing or altering the observation level is recorded in the clinical and nursing notes.

M30.7 There are regular clinical audits of the use of supportive observation and the results are discussed with all members of the multi-professional team.

Managing Disturbed Behaviour

OUTCOME

Patients displaying aggressive and violent behaviour are managed appropriately.

STANDARD M31

M31.1 There is a specific individual treatment plan for all patients who are seriously disturbed for more than a short period, which is recorded in the multi-professional patient notes.

M31.2 The policies for dealing with disturbed behaviour includes the levels of observation to be used and the degree of restriction required.

M31.3 The degree of restriction is communicated and acted upon by all staff involved in patient care.

M31.4 Where a staff member has been threatened or attacked by a patient, where possible any immediate decision about that patient's treatment plan is taken by other members of the clinical team.

M31.5 Any major changes in the treatment of disturbed or potentially violent patients (including changes of medication) are communicated to all nursing staff who have contact with the patient. Responsibility for this belongs to the registered nurse in charge at the start of the shift.

M31.6 Facilities are available for the separate care of seriously disturbed patients and where this is not possible they are nursed separately from other patients. If this involves the use of seclusion see M42.

M31.7 There are written policies and procedures for staff in relation to responding to patients who:

- refuse to participate in therapeutic programmes;
- verbally abuse and/or threaten physical harm to others; or
- destroy communal property.

Management of Serious/Untoward Incidents, Adverse Health Events and Near Misses

OUTCOME

Serious/untoward incidents, adverse health events and near misses are handled effectively and are learnt from.

STANDARD M32

M32.1 There is a written policy for serious/untoward incidents, adverse health events and near misses, which sets out the procedures to be followed with clear responsibilities for the consultant psychiatrist and the manager of the services.

M32.2 The policy:

- requires that a named individual co-ordinates the immediate response to the incident;

- sets out alarm procedures to ensure the controlled deployment of staff in response to an incident;

- includes a procedure for any person who has been seriously injured not to be left unattended by a medical practitioner or trained registered nurse for any period, however short, in any circumstances;

- sets out the process for organising any investigation and audit;

- sets out the procedures for communicating the nature of the incident at the earliest possible time to:

  – senior clinicians and managers;

  – the police; and

  – the family of the patient.

M32.3 There are immediate and ongoing support systems in place for staff and patients following a serious/untoward incident, adverse health event or near miss .

M32.4 There is a review following a the incident, within timescales set by the organisation.

M32.5 A named individual is responsible for co-ordinating the review, who is not directly involved in the management of the part of the service concerned.

M32.6 The review of the incident includes the whole multi-professional care team meeting to discuss the clinical and managerial issues which led to the particular incident.

M32.7 Patients, carers and their families and any victims are involved in the review at an early stage to ascertain their views and receive information.

M32.8 The review findings and report include recommendations for changes in practice.

M32.9 All relevant parties are informed of progress and of the outcome of the review as far as is appropriate.

M32.10 Violent incidents are audited, and any necessary redeployment of resources or other action is identified.

Unexpected Patient Death

OUTCOME

The families and carers of patients who die unexpectedly, and the staff who were involved in their care, are supported sensitively.

STANDARD M33

M33.1 There are arrangements in place for informing the patient's family members and carers following a patient's death.

M33.2 Support and information is provided to family members and carers following an unexpected patient death.

M33.3 There are arrangements in place to support staff following an unexpected patient death.

M33.4 There is a procedure in place for an investigation into the death to be instigated.

M33.5 The registered person informs the Mental Health Act Commission of the death of detained patients, date of inquiry and inquest.

M33.6 Management and members of internal investigating teams are trained in the investigative process, so that they understand the stages of investigation.

Patients Absconding

OUTCOME

All attempts are made to prevent absconding. When patients do so, effective arrangements are in place to handle the absconding.

STANDARD M34

M34.1 There are written policies and procedures, reviewed at least every three years, for dealing with patients absconding.

M34.2 There is information for patients requesting their co-operation in informing staff of their whereabouts at all times.

M34.3 Missing patient procedures are jointly agreed between services and the police and are regularly reviewed, and include guidance on reporting a patient's absence and informing the National Care Standards Commission.

M34.4 Services record levels of absconding and formally review them annually, and following any significant increase in number or the absconding of a high-risk patient. Reviews explore the reasons for absconding and ways of minimising recurrence.

Patient Restraint and Physical Interventions

OUTCOME
Patients are restrained appropriately and safely.

STANDARD M35

M35.1 There are written policies and procedures on using restraint and physical interventions with patients; if the policy is not to use restraint or physical intervention this is documented.

M35.2 The policy includes procedures for rapid tranquillisation and emergency medication.

M35.3 Staff receive training on the prevention of violence and aggression including de-escalation techniques.

M35.3 Procedures are explicit that patients are not restrained using mechanical restraints.

M35.4 All clinical areas have resources to minimise/intervene in episodes of violence or dangerous behaviour and staff are aware of these and the procedures for use.

M35.5 Patient mix, environment and staffing levels are reviewed to minimise incidents of disturbed behaviour requiring the use of physical intervention techniques.

M35.6 Physical intervention procedures are reviewed to ensure that they are employed appropriately by the full clinical team.

M35.7 When it has been necessary for a patient to be restrained a full nursing and medical review, including a physical examination, is carried out as soon as practicable.

M35.8 There is an up-to-date register of staff who have completed courses in restraint and physical intervention.

M35.9 The number, duration and form of restraint of patients is recorded and included on documentation available to the National Care Standards Commission.

Child and Adolescent Mental Health Services (additional standards)

Safeguarding Children

OUTCOME

Child and adolescent patients are treated and cared for at all times by professionals appropriately skilled, qualified and trained, whose practice conforms to regulations and guidelines issued by the various professional bodies and is based on safeguarding the interests and rights of the patients in their care.

STANDARD M36

M36.1 **There is a written policy to reflect the guidance set out in Working Together to Safeguard Children (1999), to include staff recruitment, professional qualifications and the use of police checks. This includes Protection of Children Act (POCA) checks and staff responsibility to report to the POCA list where necessary.**

M36.2 A copy of the child protection policy, compiled in collaboration with the local Area Child Protection Committee (ACPC), is available. The provision of training, on induction and thereafter annually, in child protection procedures is mandatory. A designated person for child protection is identified.

M36.3 Routine reference collection before interview, and police checks prior to appointment, are required for all staff with substantial access to children.

M36.4 Staff with a professional regulatory body (eg the Nurses and Midwives Council, the Council for Professions Supplementary to Medicine or the GMC) are checked for appropriate registration on recruitment and again at renewal date.

M36.5 There is a written policy for handling serious/untoward incidents, adverse health events and near misses and the circumstances under which reports need to be made. Such incidents and any allegations of abuse, are reported at once to the local child protection team and to the National Care Standards Commission.

Admission and Assessment

OUTCOME

Children are appropriately admitted to, and treated in, the establishment.

STANDARD M37

M37.1 The registered person informs the Local Authority if a child remains or is likely to remain an inpatient for a period of over three months (in line with section 85 of the Children Act 1989).

Quality of Life

OUTCOME

The care provided recognises the psychological, social and personal needs of children.

STANDARD M38

M38.1 There is a pre-planned programme and a pre-admission visit to allay anxiety on the part of the child, where appropriate.

M38.2 All children are admitted to a single room unless there is a specific request/clinical reason to share on a companion basis.

M38.3 A structured therapeutic programme is run during the day.

M38.4 Consideration is given to the management of mixed sex groups.

M38.5 There is a policy on restriction of liberty which is guided by the relevant criteria set out in the Mental Health Act Code of Practice 1999, and in the Children Act 1989 Guidance and Regulations, Volume 4, Chapter 8 on Secure Accommodation.

M38.6 The special needs of, and specific services for, children from different ethnic, cultural or religious backgrounds are reflected in local policies, as appropriate to the patient population.

M38.7 Children are kept in hospital only if their needs cannot be met at home, and they are discharged as soon as possible.

Facilities and Equipment to Meet the Needs of Children

OUTCOME

Appropriate facilities and equipment are used to provide treatment and care for children.

STANDARD M39

M39.1 **Children are seen in a separate outpatient area or, where the establishment does not have a separate outpatient area for children, they are seen promptly and preferably at the beginning of the session.**

M39.2 The outpatient area is subject to the same environmental audit as any other area used for children to ensure that the area is safe, with any identified risks to children controlled.

M39.3 Adolescents are to have their privacy respected, and every effort is made to respect their wishes if they indicate they prefer to be seen without their parents (bearing in mind that there may be clinical need for close family involvement).

M39.4 The toys provided are safe (compliant with British Safety Standards), and are age appropriate to the child.

M39.5 Education programmes are in place for children/young people whose length of stay exceeds five days. The programmes are managed by qualified teachers and are adequate to meet the patient's needs

Valid Consent of Children

OUTCOME

Children and their families are fully aware of, and are asked to consent to, the treatment they are to receive.

STANDARD M40

M40.1 **Clinicians speak with children and their families to ensure that children are fully aware of the treatment they are to receive.**

M40.2 A parent can give permission for treatment but the child is to be told what is happening in language appropriate to his/her level of understanding (as defined in the Mental Health Act Code of Practice 1999, chapter 31).

M40.3 The Medical practitioner obtaining consent ensures that sufficient time is allowed to explain to the parent and child the proposed procedure and allow both the opportunity to ask questions.

M40.4 Older children and adolescents are able to refuse treatment and have their concerns listened to (as defined in the Mental Health Act Code of Practice 1999, chapter 31).

M40.5 Where a child's refusal for treatment is being overruled, it is done on the basis that the welfare of the child is paramount and every effort is made to obtain his/her co-operation in these circumstances.

M40.6 The right of a young person over the age of 16 years to sign his/her own consent form is recognised.

Establishments in which Treatment or Nursing (or both) are Provided for Persons Liable to be Detained

Information for Staff

OUTCOME

Detained patients receive care and treatment in line with the Mental Health Act 1983, its consequential regulations and its Code of Practice together with the MHA Memorandum, and Mental Health Act Commission Practice Notes.

STANDARD M41

M41.1 There are written policies and procedures covering all the statutory functions of the hospital managers, reviewed at least every three years.

M41.2 Copies of the following documents are available in each of the clinical areas:

- Mental Health Act 1983;
- Mental Health (Hospital, Guardianship and Consent to Treatment) Regulations 1983;
- Mental Health (After Care Under Supervision) Regulations 1996;
- Mental Health (Patients in the Community) (Transfers from Scotland) Regulations;
- Mental Health Act Code of Practice;
- Mental Health (Patients in the Community) Act 1995 – Guidance on Supervised Discharge and Related Provisions;
- MHA 1983 Memorandum on Parts 1 to V1, VIII and X;
- Mental Health Act Commission Guidance Notes.

M41.3 There are written policies and procedures for the assessment, care, treatment and discharge of detained patients, which are drafted in accordance with the most recent version of the Code of Practice, and include policies on:

- personal searches;

- patients' correspondence;
- medical practitioners' and nurses' holding powers (Section 5 of the Act);
- patients presenting with particular management problems, including the use of seclusion;
- physical restraint;
- psychological treatments, including 'time out';
- review of treatment (Section 61 of the Act);
- patients concerned with criminal proceedings;
- leave of absence;
- absence without leave;
- the re-taking of a detained patient in the community;
- Mental Health Review Tribunals;
- managers' hearings;
- the giving of information to detained patients;
- treatment requiring the patient's consent or a second opinion (Section 58 of the Act);
- urgent treatment (Section 62 of the Act). (To be read in conjunction with standard m37.5 for young people under the age of 18.)

M41.4 The policies and procedures for services for detained patients are reviewed at least every three years.

M41.5 Guidelines for assessment of patients for admission under the Mental Health Act, which spell out the roles of all involved, are jointly developed, implemented and reviewed regularly.

M41.6 A form is completed by the responsible medical practitioner every time urgent treatment is given under Section 62 of the Mental Health Act 1983.

M41.7 The use of Section 62 is regularly monitored by managers.

M 41.8 Staff are aware of their obligations under the Mental Health Review Tribunal Regulations to produce timely and appropriate reports and to be available to give evidence at a tribunal.

M 41.9 Appropriate accommodation is made available for Mental Health Review Tribunal, hearings, including appropriate facilities for witnesses, and with due regard to the need for confidentiality.

The Rights of Patients under the Mental Health Act

> **OUTCOME**
>
> Patients and their nearest relatives are able to exercise their rights and entitlements under the Mental Health Act 1983 and its Code of Practice.

STANDARD M42

M42.1 **Detained patients and their nearest relatives are made aware of their rights and entitlements under the Mental Health Act 1983 and its Code of Practice.**

M42.2 Written information is produced, displayed and disseminated to all new patients and, subject to the patient's consent, given to their nearest relative about:

- the patient's current legal position;
- the patient's right to apply to a Mental Health Review Tribunal and request a manager's review;
- the role and function of the Mental Health Act Commission (this may be through the availability of the Mental Health Act Commission's leaflets for detained patients);
- the availability of solicitors recognised by the Law Society as being proficient in mental health work.

M42.3 There is a written policy and procedure, reviewed at least every three years, detailing the implementation of Part IV of the 1983 Mental Health Act (see M 16.2).

Seclusion of Patients

> **OUTCOME**
>
> Patients are secluded in accordance with the requirements of the 1983 Mental Health Act Code of Practice.

STANDARD M43

M43.1 **There are written policies and procedures on seclusion which are consistent with the Mental Health Act Code of Practice.**

M43.2 The written policies include guidance on:

- minimising the use of seclusion;
- the roles of professionals in initiation and review;
- monitoring by care teams and senior management;
- the appropriate use of seclusion;
- not removing the patient's clothing during or following an incident;
- the presence of same sex staff.

M43.3 Each episode of seclusion is reviewed by professionals independent of those staff in direct contact with the patient.

M43.4 Where a patient in seclusion has been sedated a registered nurse remains in sight and sound of the patient and vital signs are recorded at regular intervals.

M43.5 Rooms used for seclusion:

- provide privacy from other patients;
- enable staff to observe the patient at all times;
- do not contain anything which could cause harm to the patient or others;
- are comfortably furnished and lit;
- have controllable heating and ventilation;
- are quiet but not soundproofed and includes a means of calling for attention.

M43.6 A quarterly report of episodes of seclusion is produced for senior management and the Mental Health Act Commission, with a brief explanation of each occasion.

Section 17 Leave

OUTCOME

Arrangements for Section 17 leave of absence are appropriate and clear, and in accordance with the requirements of the 1983 Mental Health Act Code of Practice and Mental Health Act Commission Guidance Note.

STANDARD M44

M44.1 There are written policies and procedures for detained patients going on Section 17 (Mental Health Act 1983) leave.

M44.2 The policies and procedures for Section 17 leave include requirements that:

- the level of the patient's co-operation with assessment and treatment is taken into account in deciding to grant leave;
- leave is not granted until the patient has been resident for sufficient time to allow an adequate risk assessment to be undertaken;
- the named nurse/escort attends the patient reviews to report on previous leave and is party to discussion about future leave.

M44.3 All conditions pertaining to the leave are recorded on the Section 17 form, including:

- whether it is escorted, including number of escorts, or unescorted;
- level of observation;
- period of leave;
- location at which the leave will be taken;
- the purpose of the leave;

- the expected date and time of return;
- any other specific conditions.

M44.4 Careful consideration is given to the choice of venue, taking account of:
- its purpose and suitability;
- the level of risk posed to the patient in that setting;
- the patient's reason for choosing it;
- public sensitivities.

M44.5 Leave is cancelled if an appropriate escort or appropriate transport are not available.

Absence Without Leave under Section 18

OUTCOME

Appropriate arrangements are made for missing patients.

STANDARD M45

M45.1 Procedures on dealing with the situation of when patients are absent without leave are appropriate and clear, and in accordance with the requirements of the 1983 Mental Health Act Code of Practice and Mental Health Act Commission Guidance Note.

M45.2 These procedures are reviewed regularly and made known to all staff.

Discharge of Detained Patients

OUTCOME

Arrangements for the discharge of detained patients are appropriate and clear, and in accordance with the requirements of the 1983 Mental Health Act Code of Practice.

STANDARD M46

M46.1 The registered person should not delegate his or her discharge function to persons who are either on the staff of the hospital or have a financial interest in it.

M46.2 Planning for discharge under s.117 of the 1983 Mental Health Act commences on admission and discharge planning meetings are attended by or receive contributions from all personnel, disciplines and agencies

M46.3 The nominated care co-ordinator under Section 117 aftercare is an experienced mental health worker, familiar with the patient, who always attends Section 117 meetings.

M46.4   When patients are discharged from medium secure units, the discharge documents include a full risk assessment which contains a description of all overt indicators of relapse and the steps to be taken in the event of a relapse.

M46.5   Discharge documents are made available to all those directly involved in providing care.

Staff Training on the Mental Health Act

OUTCOME

Patients receive care and treatment from staff trained in. and conversant with, the provisions of the 1983 Mental Health Act and its Code of Practice.

STANDARD M47

M47.1   All staff receive training on their responsibilities under the 1983 Mental Health Act and its Code of Practice and receive annual updates on aspects of mental health legislation.

M47.2   There are written policies, which are reviewed at least every three years, to guide staff in explaining to patients (and their carers/family members) their legal rights and responsibilities under the mental health legislation.

M47.3   All clinical staff receive training on Section 17 (Mental Health Act 1983) leave procedures which forms part of the induction of new staff, and are updated when necessary.

M47.4   All care staff receive training and regular updating on consent to treatment matters including compliance with part IV of the 1983 Mental Health Act.

M 47.5   All staff receive training on responsibilities as regards Mental Health Review Tribunals and patients have full access to relevant advice.

11

Hospices

Introduction to Standards H1 to H15

Section 2(3)(a)(i) of the Care Standards Act brings within the definition of 'independent hospital' establishments the main purpose of which is to provide palliative care. For ease of reference, such establishments are described in these standards as hospices.

There are two key factors in the provision and the regulation of palliative care services. First, the need to respond to issues with a sense of urgency as time is limited for the patient nearing the end of their life. Second, the often complex and diverse needs of both the patient and their carers need to be met by access to a multi-professional specialist palliative care team with a range of skills to assist with physical, psychological, social and religious and cultural needs. The attached standards reflect this.

The standards are divided into two sections. The first section covers standards that relate both to adult and children's hospices. These standards encompass palliative care services in a range of settings: inpatient, community (ie out-reach services provided by the establishment) and day therapy. Commissioned by the Department of Health, the standards have been developed by the National Council for Hospices, and will be closely linked with the development of NICE guidance on supportive and palliative care. The second section contains additional standards that apply to children's hospices only.

The standards that relate specifically to children's palliative care services are based on the principle that a dying child is a child first and foremost, and their needs as children should be accommodated as a priority. The environment therefore needs to be child friendly and as 'home like' as possible. Many of the conditions the children have progress slowly over a number of years, placing an enormous strain on family life. A children's hospice aims to help families with this burden of care.

The standards also recognise the importance of the presence of the child's family and the need to take account of the family's wishes, and that a child's needs for play, education and contact with peers of their own age are essential components of an holistic palliative care approach.

[See: Report of the Joint Working Party of the Association for Children with Life Threatening or Terminal Conditions and their Families, the National Council for Hospice and Specialist Palliative Care Services and the Scottish Partnership Agency for Palliative and Cancer Care *Palliative Care for Young People* (2001).]

See also, in particular, regulations 33 and 36 of the Private and Voluntary Health Care Regulations.

Hospices Generally

Arrangements for Care

OUTCOME
Patients and prospective patients, their families and carers, are clear about the arrangements for palliative care.

STANDARD H1

H1.1 Written information is provided about eligibility criteria for the treatment and care being provided and how to access this.

H1.2 Information about eligibility criteria and access is made widely available to referring bodies.

H1.3 The referral process is clearly described and response times to new referrals regularly reviewed to ensure there are no delays in gaining access.

H1.4 Patients are discharged with all the identified support services in place.

H1.5 Hospices providing a community service and care at home have a lone worker safety policy.

Palliative Care Expertise and Training for Multi-professional Teams

OUTCOME
Patients are cared for by people who have the relevant expertise.

STANDARD H2

H2.1 Staff with specialist palliative care expertise function in multi-professional teams to ensure that the palliative care needs of patients and carers are met.

H2.2 Multi-professional palliative care teams are recruited, developed, educated and trained for the services which the provider is registered to undertake.

H2.3 The multi-professional team membership is commensurate with the service being provided.

H2.4   There is a multi-professional team meeting at least weekly for patient management, with arrangements in place for ethical decision making and patient advocacy where this is indicated and required.

H2.5   Formal, multi-professional team meetings are held at least annually with other related agencies or services for audit, service operation and communication review.

H2.6   All members of the multi-professional team are trained in the assessment of palliative care needs across the dimensions of physical, psychological, social, religious and cultural needs.

H2.7   All team members are trained in the provision of general psychological care for patients and carers.

H2.8   All team members are able to communicate with patients and their carers with sensitivity, ensuring that patients and their carers receive all the information they want concerning their condition, treatment and care.

H2.9   All team members have received training and updating in communication skills and the breaking of bad news.

H2.10   There are in place systems of both professional and personal support for all those who work in the establishment.

Assessment of Patients' and Carers' Needs

OUTCOME

The needs of patients and carers are appropriately assessed.

STANDARD H3

H3.1   Patients' and carers' needs are assessed by a member of the multi-professional team.

H3.2   The assessment covers all domains, including:

- physical;
- psychological;
- social;
- religious and spiritual;
- cultural.

H3.3   Treatment and care choices are clearly explained to patients and carers with sufficient information, time and assistance to make informed decisions, and to give informed consent where appropriate.

H3.4   The patient and carer assessment is subject to review as and when changes in care are indicated.

Delivery of Palliative Care

OUTCOME

Patients receive appropriate palliative care.

STANDARD H4

H4.1 **A member of the multi-professional team is designated as the principal contact for each patient and carer.**

H4.2 A member of the multi-professional team is identified who will provide access to agencies or services for carer support including bereavement support.

H4.3 Information about carer support services and how they may be accessed is easily accessible in a variety of formats and places.

H4.4 There are procedures for patients and carers, and for those who work in the establishment, for accessing out-of-hours specialist advice and support.

H4.5 Care pathways are in place which delineate the care to be provided to patients and their carers and which are used as a part of clinical audit and outcomes analysis.

H4.6 The multi-professional team employ evidence-based clinical guidelines.

H4.7 Arrangements are in place for regularly and systematically obtaining patient and carer views about their experience of using palliative care services from the provider.

H4.8 The environment in which care is given affords patients and carers the privacy they require and enables them to be treated with dignity at all times.

H4.9 Care and services are delivered in such a manner as to be patient- and carer-centred, taking into account patient and carer preferences and requests.

H4.10 The care of the patient after death takes into account all religious and cultural requirements, and the requests of both the patient and family.

Records of Care

OUTCOME

Patient care is based upon accurate records.

STANDARD H5

H5.1 **Members of the multi-professional team have continuous access to up-to-date records and other information about patients and their carers.**

H 5.2 All team members keep patient records up to date following each patient/carer contact.

H5.3 There is access to an information system capable of supporting service review.

H5.4 Communications between team members and services are concise and in a language which is readily comprehensible between professionals.

Infection Control

OUTCOME

The risk of patients, staff and visitors acquiring a health care-associated infection is minimised.

STANDARD H6

H6.1 There are formal links and membership of an infection control team; this may be within another organisation, such as a local acute services NHS Trust.

H6.2 There is a registered nurse with designated responsibilities for infection control that are included in a documented job description and there is a defined time commitment for infection control activities.

H6.3 The infection control link nurse has training in infection control and provides evidence of continuing professional development (CPD) in relation to the role in infection control.

H6.4 Prevention and control of infection are considered as part of all proposed service developments.

H6.5 Written policies, procedures and guidance for the prevention and control of infection are implemented and reflect relevant legislation and published professional guidance, including:

- major outbreaks of communicable infections;
- isolation of patients;
- antimicrobial prescribing;
- control of MRSA, VRE and other antimicrobial resistant micro-organisms;
- control of tuberculosis, including multi-drug resistant tuberculosis;
- collection, packaging, handling and delivery of laboratory specimens;
- handling of medical devices in procedures carried out on known/suspect CJD patients and on patients in risk categories for CJD as defined in the ACDP/SEAC guidance (including disposal/quarantining procedures).

H6.6 Each department or service has a current copy of the approved policies, procedures and guidelines pertinent to its activities.

Resuscitation

OUTCOME

Patients' rights are observed around the issue of resuscitation.

STANDARD H7

H7.1 Information about the hospice's resuscitation policy is available for patients.

H7.2 The registered person must ensure that patients' rights are central to decision-making on resuscitation.

H7.3 The policy includes appropriate supervision arrangements to review resuscitation decisions.

H7.4 Health care professionals with a thorough understanding of the resuscitation policy and its application are on duty at all times and are available to make resuscitation decisions.

Responsibility for Pharmaceutical Services

OUTCOME

Responsibility for obtaining, prescribing, storing, use, handling, recording and disposal of medicines is clear.

STANDARD H8

H8.1 The medical director or senior registered nurse is responsible for safe medicines systems, unless there is a pharmacy department supplying medicines within the same body corporate as the hospice, when the senior pharmacist will be responsible.

H8.2 The hospice has a ward/clinical pharmacy service and pharmacist medicines information service.

Ordering, Storage, Use and Disposal of Medicines

OUTCOME

Medicines, dressings and gases are handled in a safe and secure manner.

STANDARD H9

H9.1 **All medicines, medical gases and interactive wound dressings are obtained by, and stored under the control of, the senior registered nurse, or medical director under the control of the senior nurse, or the pharmacist.**

H9.2 The pharmacist or, where there is no pharmacist employed, the senior registered nurse or medical director, authorises any orders to obtain prescription-only medicines from wholesale suppliers.

H9.3 Stocks of medicines in current use on the unit or ward are the responsibility of the senior registered nurses designated for the purpose by the registered nurse manager.

H9.4 A medication record is kept for each patient, the entries signed by the prescriber, showing:

- the name and date of birth of the patient;
- registration number and ward where appropriate;
- the name of the medicine;
- the dose;
- the route of administration;
- the frequency and time for administering each dose;
- the date of prescribing;
- any known medicines hypersensitivity or allergies;
- any special requirements.

H9.6 Records are kept for eight years from the date of discharge or death of the patient.

H9.7 Medicines brought into the hospice by individual patients, and which are not used, are kept separate from other medicines on the ward and held in a safe place until discharge of the patient when they are returned to the patient or his/her representative. A written policy should exist for the use of patients' own medicines including criteria to assess the suitability of medicines for reuse.

H9.8 The disposal of waste is carried out by an authorised contractor who is used to complying with the arrangements for pharmaceutical waste, including cytotoxic waste where appropriate.

H9.9 When a patient dies in the hospice the patient's medicines are kept for at least one week in case there is a need for a coroner's inquest.

Administration of Medicines

OUTCOME

Appropriately trained and qualified health care professionals administer all medicines and drugs to patients.

STANDARD H10

H10.1 **Medicines are administered by a registered medical practitioner or a registered nurse in accordance with the UKCC's *Guidelines for the administration of medicines* (October 2000) or by another registered professional assessed as competent to administer those medicines.**

H10.2 There is a secure method for transporting medicines from the medicines cupboard to the patient.

H10.3 When medicines are no longer required by the named patient they are returned to the pharmacy or pharmacist for disposal.

Self-administration of Medicines

OUTCOME

Patients are assessed, consulted and advised before they are enabled to self-administer medicines.

STANDARD H11

H11.1 **There is a written policy and procedure for self-medication, which conforms to the duty of care inherent in the relationship of the hospice to the patient.**

H11.2 Where the risks have been assessed and it is deemed appropriate, patients are enabled to self-administer their medicines.

H11.3 Arrangements are made only with the agreement of the senior registered nurse, the patient and the medical practitioner responsible for the patient's care.

H11.4 Medicines dispensed for patients to self-administer have full directions and BNF cautionary warning where appropriate.

H11.5 Regular checks are made on the quantity of medicine given to the patient to ensure the patient is not taking higher doses of medicine than prescribed.

H11.6 The medicine is stored in a personal lockable cupboard or drawer, the keys being held by the patient.

H11.7 There is a spare key to which health care staff have access.

Storage and Supply of Medical Gases

> **OUTCOME**
>
> Medical gases are stored and supplied appropriately.

STANDARD H12

H12.1 **Where piped medical gases are used there is a named Authorised Person MGPS (medical gas pipeline systems) responsible for the storage, identification, quality and purity of all gases at the terminal units, and for maintaining gas pipelines, and compliance with HTM 2022; this may be an appropriately qualified employee or through a contract with a medical gas company.**

H12.2 Where the Authorised Person is not employed on site at the hospital there is a named member of staff delegated to be his representative on the site as the Quality Controller of the medical gas pipeline system; this person must have training and familiarity with medical gas systems.

H12.3 Prior to use of a new system, or resumption of use of a repaired system, the named quality controller is required to indicate that he or she is satisfied with the operation of the pipelines system and the identity and purity of the gases at terminal units alongside the signature of the Authorised Person who accepts responsibility of the correct operation of the pipeline systems.

H12.4 Any engineers (competent persons) delegated to work on the medical gas pipelines systems have training and are authorised to do so by the Authorised Person.

H12.5 All work on medical gas pipeline systems is controlled by a permit to work procedure, which includes ensuring that all paperwork with respect to work carried out on the medical gas pipeline system is copied to the Authorised Person.

H12.6 Policies and procedures are produced for recording the delivery, handling and storage of full and empty medical gas cylinders, with an indication of who is in charge of this procedure at each site.

Additional Standards for Children's Hospices

Assessment and Care of Children

OUTCOME

The special needs of children are addressed.

STANDARD H13

H13.1 The child and family's needs are assessed (prior to admission if possible) and a care plan is developed, which is updated when required.

H13.2   The assessment process includes the child's developmental and educational needs.

H13.3   The child and parents are included in any discussions and decisions about treatment and care, and choices are explained with sufficient information, time and assistance to make informed decisions, and to give informed consent where appropriate.

H14.4   Care staff recognise the unique wishes of each child and their family and accommodate these and the child's daily routine in an individualised care plan which is agreed with the family and, where possible, with the child.

H13.5   The child's care plan is reviewed on each visit to the hospice or during each episode of care in the community, but also updated as and when changes in care are indicated.

H13.6   Where children are cared for, the services provided are child and family-centred and promote a child orientated routine.

H13.7   The treatment and care provided encourages parental involvement in their child's care.

H13.8   The treatment and care promotes a child centred routine with regard to sleeping and feeding requirements, and there is sufficient flexibility to accommodate individual children's usual pattern of daily care.

H13.9   The child and parents are kept informed about the child's condition.

H13.10 In partnership with parents, information is provided to the child and siblings about treatment and care which is appropriate to their age, understanding and the specific circumstances.

H13.11 Symptom control is used to promote comfort and enhance quality of life of the child. (Symptom control means the management of any/all symptoms a child may experience in order to promote comfort and enhance the quality of life. Symptom control is much more than simply pain relief, although this is an important feature of symptom control.)

H13.12 Symptom control is evaluated, at least daily, by a member of the multi-professional team.

H13.13 The evaluation of symptom control involves the family, and where necessary other agencies contributing to the care of the child and family.

H13.14 The symptom control and evaluation takes account of the particular vulnerabilities of children with sensory impairment and those who are unable to communicate.

H13.15 The care of the child both before and after death respects the wishes of both the child and family and takes into account religious and cultural requirements.

H13.16 When death occurs within the children's hospice, there is a room with suitable facilities for the child's body to remain until the time of the funeral if that is the parents' wish.

H13.17 The family are offered accommodation at the hospice during this period and a designated team member should be made available to give sensitive emotional support and information about, or practical help with, organising the funeral and any other aspects relating to the death.

H13.18 Bereavement care is offered in accordance with the wishes of the family which includes bereavement support for siblings.

H13.19 Staff communicate regularly and work in close co-operation with all other statutory or voluntary health care workers involved in the care of the child and family.

Qualifications and Training for Staff Caring for Children

OUTCOME

Children are cared for by appropriately qualified and trained staff.

STANDARD H14

H14.1 The multi-professional team at a children's hospice is led by a qualified children's nurse with a further qualification in paediatric palliative care and/or experience in the palliative care of children and young people.

H14.2 There are arrangements in place for on-call medical cover at all times. (Preferably by a medical practitioner with training and expertise in paediatrics and palliative care, but, if not, access to this expertise must be available at all times.)

H14.3 There is a communication policy agreed with the Health Authorities and NHS Trusts whence the children come, to include frequency of multi-professional meetings with staff inside and outside the hospice.

H14.4 Staff have training to recognise the vulnerability of ill children, including in the following areas:

- child protection;
- assessing pain and discomfort;
- how the child asserts his/her own best interests.

H14.5   Staff are trained to understand the communication needs of children according to their age and ability, and any disability they may have.

H14.6   There is a minimum of one children's nurse on duty at all times.

H14.7   There are sufficient numbers of children's nurses employed to allow two children's nurses to be available for each shift in 24-hours if necessary.

H14.8   There is flexibility in how children's nurses are deployed, allowing them to be rostered according to the needs of children.

H14.9   Staff are trained in the calculation and administration of medicines to children, and those staff are the only ones allowed to check drugs for children.

H14.10 All care staff are trained in the assessment of the child across the dimensions of physical, psychological, social, developmental, educational, spiritual and cultural needs.

H14.11 All staff are trained in supporting families when there are decisions about treatment and end of life care to be made.

H14.12 All staff are aware of sources of advice and guidance regarding ethical dilemmas.

Environment for Care of Children

OUTCOME

Children's special needs are addressed by the facilities provided.

STANDARD H15

H15.1   The establishment is furnished and equipped to meet the needs of children and young people, with particular efforts made to minimise the clinical and institutional environment and to promote a homely and welcoming setting.

H15.2   Accommodation is provided for the child's family, including siblings, and unrestricted parental involvement in the child's care is promoted.

H15.3   Children are cared for alongside other children and their play and educational needs are met.

H15.4   Arrangements are made to ensure that:

- qualified play staff are employed;

- indoor and outdoor play areas are accessible to all (including children in wheelchairs);

- there is a wide variety of play equipment to meet the needs of infants and children of different ages, developmental stages and differing intellectual abilities and to help them express their feelings and prepare for experiences ahead.

H15.5 There is access to teaching staff and educational facilities, and equipment for all children aged between five and 16 years, including provision for those with special educational needs.

H15.6 Children and young people should be cared for alongside children in similar peer groups and not in a facility unsuitable for their age.

H15.7 Provision is made to meet the needs of children with disabilities.

H15.8 Meals are a family occasion, centred on a communal dining area with a varied menu. Choice of where to take meals is also available.

H15.9 A children's menu is available which meets current nutritional advice and can be adapted for children of different age groups in terms of size, content and timing of meals.

H15.10 The children's menu should cater for the tastes and preferences of children and accommodate special diets for cultural and medical purposes.

H15.11 Cutlery and utensils are available which suit the needs of children of different ages and abilities.

H15.12 Planning of the environment for children includes preventing access by a child to hot surfaces, hot water, storage of cleaning materials, and access to power points.

H15.13 All staff are made aware of their responsibility to protect children.

H15.14 Staff are alert to the presence of strangers and establish their identity immediately.

H15.15 The children's hospice is secured at night.

12

Maternity Hospitals

Introduction to Standards MC1 to MC8

Section 2(7)(c) of the Care Standards Act brings within the definition of 'independent hospitals' establishments in which obstetric services and/or, in connection with childbirth, medical services are provided. For ease of reference, such establishments are described in these standards as maternity hospitals. For maternity hospitals that are also acute hospitals these standards need to be applied alongside the acute hospital standards.

The attached standards reflect that the important factors in ensuring patients receive safe and effective maternity services (including antenatal care, delivery, post-natal care and the care of the newborn baby) are:

- recognition of the special nature of the clinical care involved;
- ensuring that those involved in providing the services are appropriately qualified and trained;
- recognition of the role of general practitioners, midwives and obstetricians;
- ensuring that urgent and emergency procedures can take place quickly and safely;
- ensuring that routine and special needs of the mother and the newborn baby are met.

See also, in particular, regulations 39 and 40 of the Private and Voluntary Health Care Regulations.

Maternity Services

Human Resources

> **OUTCOME**
>
> Patients receive treatment from properly qualified and trained health care professionals.

STANDARD MC1

MC1.1 **Obstetricians, gynaecologists and anaesthetists are current Members or Fellows of their respective medical Royal Colleges, have sufficient experience and seniority and be in good standing. They are also on the specialist register of the General Medical Council.**

MC1.2 Midwives are registered with the Nurses and Midwives Council and have notified her/his intention to practice to the Local Supervising Authority. A Head of Midwifery is appointed in all maternity units.

MC1.3 All midwives take part in a Continuing Professional Development programme which satisfies their Nurses and Midwives Council requirements for Post Registration Education and Practice (PREP). This is checked on a three yearly basis.

MC1.4 Gynaecologists undertaking laparoscopic surgery and sterilisation have undergone accredited updated training in relevant special skills modules as developed by the Royal College of Obstetricians and Gynaecologists (RCOG). (RCOG Minimal Access Criterion Levels 1-3).

MC1.5 All midwives have access to a Supervisor of Midwives, who in turn should have access to the unit to ensure the maintenance of midwifery standards.

MC1.6 All health care professionals attend regular multi-disciplinary education/training sessions.

Infection Control

> **OUTCOME**
>
> The risk of patients, staff and visitors acquiring a health care-associated infection is minimised.

STANDARD MC 2

MC2.1 **Written policies, procedures and guidance for the prevention and control of infection are implemented and reflect relevant legislation and published professional guidance, addressing:**

- **major outbreaks of communicable infections; and**
- **isolation of patients.**

Records Management

OUTCOME

Patients treatment is informed by effective and accurate records.

STANDARD MC3

MC3.1 The type of delivery is recorded in the maternity notes.

MC3.2 Numbers of caesarean sections performed by individual consultants are kept and regularly audited.

MC3.3 There are storage facilities to keep the records traceable and secure against loss, damage or use by unauthorised persons.

Antenatal Care

OUTCOME

Patients receive safe and effective antenatal care.

STANDARD MC4

MC4.1 Antenatal care and antenatal screening tests and their quality standards comply with the standards detailed in the antenatal screening programme of the National Screening Committee, the Royal College of Obstetricians and Gynaecologists guidelines 'Effective Procedures in Maternity Care suitable for Audit' and with any guidelines from the National Institute of Clinical Excellence (NICE) concerning pregnancy and delivery.

MC4.2 Antenatal screening tests are performed only with the woman's informed consent following a pre-test discussion with the woman, preferably together with her partner.

MC4.3 Women who choose to be screened, for whatever condition, have the results conveyed to them as soon as possible.

MC4.4 Potentially adverse results from screening tests are given in person within 48 hours of the result becoming available, enabling counselling and support to be provided. All women and their partners are offered counselling whatever their reproductive choice or the outcome.

MC4.5 Care programmes for women who are likely to refuse blood products are drawn up during pregnancy and written in the notes. Advance care directives are also obtained in these cases. Clinical guidelines in the Confidential Enquiries into Maternal Deaths (CEMD) Report are followed.

MC4.6 All women receive advice about signs and symptoms of problems such as pre-eclampsia or early labour and have a telephone contact number for a named person employed by the clinic or hospital, readily contactable at all times.

MC4.7 There are written procedures for Anti-D to be routinely used to prevent or minimise the risk of rhesus iso-immunisation for all rhesus negative pregnant women, as a minimum, following any possible sensitising event during pregnancy, and immediately after birth.

Additional Standards for Midwife-led Units

OUTCOME

Midwife-led units have effective arrangements to ensure the safety of the mother and her baby.

STANDARD MC5

MC5.1 Patients who choose to be cared for solely by a midwife practitioner are assessed to ascertain if there are likely to be any complications at a later stage and these are explained to them.

MC5.2 In midwife-led units, protocols for the identification and screening out of women at higher risk of complications, or operative delivery with subsequent transfer to a consultant unit for the remainder of their care, are in place together with protocols for the emergency transfer of women with sudden or unexpected complications.

MC5.3 Women at anticipated higher risk of complications but who refuse advice to be transferred to medically-led care are fully informed of the possible adverse consequences to both themselves and the fetus of this action. A written and signed record of the decision is kept.

MC5.4 There is a written evidence-based referral protocol to obstetric consultant care for women at recognised risk of complications.

MC5.5 In a midwife-led unit, a registered midwife who has notified her intention to practice to the Local Supervising Authority is available on-call throughout the 24-hour period, and available to attend within 15 minutes of being summoned.

MC5.6 At all times when there are women receiving care in the establishment a midwife is on duty.

MC5.7 Midwife-led units have in place agreed protocols for the management of obstetric and neonatal emergencies which include emergency access to an appropriately experienced obstetrician and/or paediatrician. At least one midwife who has undertaken the Advanced Life Support in Obstetrics (ALSO) course, or similar, is on duty at all times.

Childbirth

OUTCOME

Effective arrangements are in place for the safe delivery of the mother and her baby.

STANDARD MC6

MC6.1 There are written, referenced, evidence-based, multi-disciplinary policies for the management of all key conditions/situations on the antenatal and post-natal wards and the delivery suite. These are subject to review at intervals of not more than three years. They include written policies for all the conditions described in the latest Clinical Negligence Scheme for Trusts (CNST) Report.

MC6.2 All health care professionals agree and adhere to these policies, ensuring that no confusion arises over individual deviations in practice should an emergency arise.

MC6.3 Arrangements are in place for the prompt supply of blood products in emergency situations. Regular drills take place to check the adequacy of the arrangements.

MC6.4 Arrangements are in place for the prompt transfer of women/babies requiring intensive or other specialist care. A medical practitioner, midwife or neonatal nurse accompanies the mother, baby or both.

MC6.5 A consultant obstetrician is readily contactable in an emergency and, taking into account local circumstances, is able to arrive within 15 minutes of being contacted.

MC6.6 Apart from in midwife-led units, caesarean section is undertaken rapidly and in a short enough period to eliminate unacceptable delay. When a decision is made to perform an emergency caesarean section, the person taking the decision indicates clearly the urgency with which it needs to be carried out. The time from the decision to operate until the start of operation does not normally exceed 30 minutes.

MC6.7 Each obstetric unit with a significant number of deliveries must have critical care beds where patients are cared for by an experienced midwife.

MC6.8 In the case of adverse health events and near misses, including critical incidents, maternal or neonatal deaths or stillbirths, a local enquiry takes place as well as a multi-disciplinary risk management assessment.

MC6.9 When an adverse health event or near miss occurs, report forms are filled in by all staff involved within 24 hours.

Maternal Death or Stillbirth

OUTCOME

Maternal deaths or stillbirths are dealt with sensitively and are reported appropriately.

STANDARD MC7

MC7.1 There is a written policy in place for action following a maternal death or a stillbirth.

MC7.2 Staff encourage parents to see/hold their baby and there are arrangements in place for photographs to be taken.

MC7.3 Suitable facilities are provided for a mother (and her family) who has undergone a stillbirth or who has a very ill baby so that she does not have to be cared for in close proximity to mothers with healthy babies.

MC7.4 Local leaders of religious faiths are readily contactable on request for the family of the mother or baby.

MC7.5 Where a maternal death, stillbirth or neonatal death takes place the following steps are taken:

- there is a local enquiry as well as the death reported to the coroner and to either the Confidential Enquiries into Maternal Deaths (CEMD) or the Confidential Enquiry into Stillbirths and Deaths in Infancy (CESDI);

- whenever possible a postmortem is performed in light of both CEMD and CESDI recommendations for good practice;

- the relatives are fully informed about the circumstances surrounding the death and have further meetings with staff at their request;

- where the patient had a thrombosis, cardiac or other possible genetically linked problems, the possibility of an inherited defect is explored and screening of the family offered if necessary; and

- ongoing bereavement counselling is made available for the family.

Care of the Newborn Baby

OUTCOME

Mothers and newborn babies receive appropriate quality treatment and screening.

STANDARD MC8

MC8.1 There is a designated consultant paediatrician with general oversight of care protocols.

MC8.2 There is emergency access to a paediatric team for support for very ill babies and for consultations on a regular basis for other problems affecting the newborn baby.

MC8.3 Emergency transfer arrangements are agreed with a local neonatal intensive care unit.

MC8.4 Arrangements are in place for the routine examination and screening of newborn babies, these include:

- routine screening for congenital hip dysplasia and metabolic/blood disorders which are subject to national screening programme standards;
- TB screening;
- immunisation for Hepatitis B, if the need for this is identified by antenatal screening;
- a policy for prevention of vitamin K deficiency bleeding taking account of national guidance.

MC8.5 Written policies are in place for the management of common problems of newborn babies including jaundice, hypoglycaemia and infection and a unit policy for the management of group B streptococcal infection.

MC8.6 Arrangements are in place for all women and babies to be transferred to the care of their local community midwives, health visitors and GPs.

MC8.7 Parents are given information on how and where to register the birth.

MC8.8 Arrangements are in place to ensure that the allocation of an NHS number at birth is made.

13

Termination of Pregnancy Establishments

Introduction to Standards TP1 to TP5

The Abortion Act 1967 as amended requires termination of pregnancy to be carried out in an NHS hospital or in a place approved for this purpose by the Secretary of State for Health. Currently, proprietors of abortion services have to undertake to comply with the Department's Required Standard Operating Principles as well as registration under the Registered Homes Act 1984, with respective inspections by both the Department of Health and the Health Authority. The introduction of the NCSC provides an opportunity to streamline the procedures for approving and monitoring abortion clinics (for instance, by delegating the Department of Health inspection duties to the NCSC).

The following standards apply to establishments in which terminations of pregnancy take place (defined as 'independent hospitals' under Section 2(7)(d) of the Care Standards Act). The standards aim to ensure that:

- services comply with the requirements of the Abortion Act (including notifications requirements);

- services comply with clinical guidelines and guidance issued by the Department of Health;

- establishments can accept termination of pregnancy referrals only from a medical practitioner or a pregnancy advice bureau;

- appropriate information is provided to those seeking or obtaining an abortion; and

- information is provided to help facilitate the inspection of services.

Women need objective sources of information about abortion and possible alternatives and should not feel pressured into proceeding with a termination. Requiring the provision of information materials and specifying when fees can be accepted are intended to reduce these pressures.

Abortions are generally day care procedures, so women tend to leave the establishment where the procedure takes place within a couple of hours. However, they may develop complications or be in pain or be anxious about how much bleeding to expect. They should therefore be given contact telephone numbers to ring for advice. It is important that the registered person records that this information has been provided. As medical abortion becomes more frequently used (ie where a woman is given tablets to terminate the pregnancy but the actual abortion occurs some time later, sometimes when the patient has returned to her own home) it is particularly important that information and support services are available.

Respect is due to the dead fetus based on its lost potential for development into a fully formed human being. Full account should be taken of any personal wishes that have been expressed about disposal of fetal tissue. All fetal tissue should be disposed of in accordance with national guidance.

See also, in particular, regulation 41 of the Private and Voluntary Health Care Regulations.

Termination of Pregnancy

Quality of Treatment and Care

OUTCOME

Patients receive quality treatment and care.

STANDARD TP1

TP1.1 **Relevant Department of Health guidance, including Department of Health** *Procedures for the Approval of Independent Sector Places for the Termination of Pregnancy* **(October 1999) is followed.**

TP1.2 Termination of pregnancy establishments ensure that no referral of a Patient for termination of pregnancy is accepted unless it is made by a medical practitioner or pregnancy advice bureaux approved by the Department of Health.

Information for Patients

OUTCOME

Patients are aware of the measures they need to take before and after treatment.

STANDARD TP2

TP2.1 **Patients are given information prior to attending for the procedure on:**

- **instructions with regard to any existing medication;**
- **travel directions to the establishment;**
- **contact telephone number for the establishment for queries prior to the procedure.**

TP2.2   On leaving the establishment each patient is provided with information about:

- post procedure pain relief;
- post procedure bleeding;
- taking care of herself after the procedure;
- possible complications;
- a telephone contact number at the establishment to ring for advice;
- a 24-hour telephone number for advice elsewhere if the establishment is not open 24 hours a day.

TP2.3   A written record is maintained which notes the information given to the patient.

Privacy and Confidentiality for Patients

OUTCOME

Patients are assured of privacy and confidentiality.

STANDARD TP3

TP3.1   All records of terminations, which include patient-attributable information, are stored securely and kept strictly confidential within the establishment.

TP3.2   The arrangements for the reception of patients and consultation with patients ensure that patient privacy is maintained at all times.

TP3.3   There are procedures for staff to follow to ensure that patient's names and personal details are not heard or seen in any public area of the establishment.

Respect for Fetal Tissue

OUTCOME

Fetal tissue is handled sensitively.

STANDARD TP4

TP4.1   There are written policies and procedures for staff to follow so that fetal tissue is treated with dignity and respect, in accordance with Department of Health guidance.

TP4.2   Procedures allow for any personal wishes expressed by the patient to be taken into consideration with regard to the disposal of fetal tissue.

TP4.3 Policies include a statement that fetal material may be supplied for research purposes only in accordance with the Polkinghorne Code of Practice and with express permission from the patient. The National Care Standards Commission should be informed about any new request to supply fetal material for research purposes.

Emergency Procedures

OUTCOME

Patients are transferred safely in cases of emergency.

STANDARD TP5

TP5.1 **There are written procedures for the transfer of patients to an inpatient bed, either within the hospital or at another establishment if this is necessary due to complications from the procedure.**

TP5.2 Where the transfer is to another establishment the arrangements are agreed with that establishment and documented.

14

Prescribed Techniques and Prescribed Technology

Introduction to Standards P1 to P16

Establishments in which treatments are provided using certain techniques and technology are regulated (until 31 March 2002) under the Registered Homes Act 1984. These are techniques or technology – such as lasers – that require expertise in delivery, the use of appropriate equipment and for the setting to have certain measures in place in order for the treatment to be delivered safely. Regulation based on these same principles will continue under the CSA.

The NCSC will maintain regulation of the techniques and technology currently regulated (although a new exemption will be introduced for Class 3B lasers where they are used by or under the supervision of registered health care professionals) *and* regulation will also be extended to include treatment using intense pulsed light sources and to hyperbaric oxygen treatment/therapy. The reasoning for this is set out below.

Class 3B and 4 Lasers and/or Intense Pulsed Light Sources (standards P1 to P3)

The standards cover both Class 3B and 4 lasers and intense pulsed lights, as these technologies share similar features. Intense pulsed lights are defined, in regulation 3 of the Private and Voluntary Health Care Regulations, as:

> *Broadband non-coherent light which is filtered to produce a specified range of wavelengths; such filtered radiation being delivered to the body with the aim of causing thermal, mechanical or chemical damage to structures such as hair follicles and skin blemishes while sparing surrounding tissues.*

Class 3B lasers are concentrated energy sources used for physiotherapy, eg to relieve chronic pain and backache by 'massaging' the tissue by pulsing the beam through it; for acupuncture; and for wound healing, for instance pressure sores, venous and diabetic ulcers, and for softening scar tissue. The majority of users are State Registered and/or Chartered Physiotherapists and Podiatrists – who will be exempted from regulation (see above).

Class 4 lasers and intense pulsed light sources are used in a variety of settings and for a variety of purposes. For instance, they are used for medical treatment in acute hospitals; in dental treatment; and in establishments ranging from clinics providing invasive cosmetic surgery by medical practitioners, to beauty salons where operators provide minimally or non-invasive cosmetic services which do not require the operator to be medically qualified. These include the removal of hair, tattoos, birthmarks or other blemishes from the skin. Class 4 lasers and intense pulsed lights are powerful devices which, if faulty or used incorrectly, have the potential to cause serious injury to those operating them, recipients of the treatment and other persons in the vicinity, and to ignite flammable materials.

It is essential, therefore, that all establishments that provide treatment using Class 3B lasers (except where the laser is used by or under the supervision of a health care professional), Class 4 lasers or intense pulsed light sources, whether for medical or cosmetic treatment, are effectively regulated by the NCSC so that recipients of treatment and those who work or come within the confines of the regulated establishment are protected from laser and intense pulsed light emissions.

We regard that the key elements in ensuring that lasers and intense pulsed lights sources are used safely centre around:

- clear lines of responsibility within the registered establishments on the use of lasers and intense pulsed lights, including a clear understanding by all users of the personal responsibility that using lasers and intense pulsed lights entails;
- clear policies and procedures on the use and maintenance of lasers and intense pulsed lights;
- users of laser and intense pulsed lights undergoing specialised training, and learning, maintaining and updating an effective core of knowledge about the use and impact of lasers and intense pulsed lights;
- effective record keeping;
- safe working areas; and
- protective eyewear and other risk-avoidance measures.

The attached standards reflect this.

See also, in particular, regulations 3 and 42 and Schedule 3 paragraph 3 of the Private and Voluntary Health Care Regulations.

Dialysis (standards P4 to P6)

Haemodialysis and peritoneal dialysis are carried out in the independent sector in a range of settings. These are, typically, acute hospitals, holiday sites (for example Butlin's and Scout Association Holiday Homes) and private satellite units where dialysis is provided under contract to the NHS. The standards do not apply to dialysis that takes place in the patient's home.

Where the NHS uses private satellite units to provide dialysis to NHS patients, these units are required to join the Renal Registry, in association with the main unit to which they are linked. The purpose of the Renal Registry is to monitor the quantity and quality of renal care in the UK. The attached standards provide added quality assurance to that process.

See also, in particular, regulation 3 of the Private and Voluntary Health Care Regulations.

Endoscopy

Premises where endoscopy takes place are currently regulated under the Registered Homes Act. These include acute hospitals and GPs' surgeries. This position is to be carried forward under the CSA.

Endoscopes are medical devices inserted in the body for diagnostic or surgical purposes. There are two types of endoscope, flexible and rigid:

- flexible endoscopy uses natural body orifices (eg mouth, anus, nose) to introduce into the body a long flexible device. The inserted end of the device has a camera, operated remotely by the practitioner, which is used to view the internal organs. These procedures usually include upper and lower gastroscopy, bronchoscopy, laryngoscopy, cystoscopy and hysteroscopy. Most acute hospitals have an endoscopy department (sometimes known as a day surgery centre) where flexible endoscopy is undertaken, but it may also take place in other health care establishments;

- rigid endoscopy is where a rigid endoscope with a surgical instrument at the inserted end is introduced through the skin. It is also known as minimally invasive surgery or keyhole surgery and includes arthroscopy, laparoscopy, hysteroscopy and cystoscopy, among others. Rigid endoscopy usually takes place in hospital operating departments.

Endoscopes are subject to standards for medical devices and, where they are re-usable, for decontamination. Standards relating to medical devices and decontamination are to be found in both the core standards and those for acute hospitals, and are therefore not duplicated here.

See also, in particular, regulation 3 of the Private and Voluntary Health Care Regulations.

Hyperbaric Oxygen Treatment/Therapy (standards P7 to P11)

Hyperbaric oxygen therapy (HBOT) involves specialised equipment and experienced personnel to deliver oxygen at higher than atmospheric pressures. The safe and judicious use of this therapy is increasing as medical and paramedical staff become familiar with its potential benefits. It is used for a number of conditions that have been demonstrated to benefit by well-established research. The European Committee for Hyperbaric Medicine (ECHM) advocates hyperbaric oxygen for the first-line treatment of the following conditions:

- air or gas embolism;
- decompression illness;
- carbon monoxide poisoning;
- gas gangrene;
- necrotising fasciitis;

- post-radiotherapy tissue damage;
- preparation for surgery in previously irradiated tissue.

In addition, the USA Undersea and Hyperbaric Medical Society (UHMS) support the use of hyperbaric oxygen for the following conditions:

- crush injury;
- severe haemorrhagic anaemia;
- selected problem wounds;
- compromised skin flaps and grafts;
- refractory osteomyelitis;
- osteoradionecrosis;
- thermal burns;
- intracranial abscess.

In 1983 the New England Journal of medicine reported a controlled, double-blind study on the effect of HBOT on the symptoms of multiple sclerosis (MS). It demonstrated benefits, but the researchers recognised the need for long-term studies. A pilot study confirmed the findings, but there have been no clinical trials published in the medical literature that have satisfied the medical establishment that HBOT is of long-term benefit to MS patients. The treatment is not, therefore, among the indications for HBOT listed above. As a result, a number of HBOT chambers have been installed by charitable treatment centres throughout the UK, including 56 owned by the MS Society, and the number of HBOT units provided by commercial and charitable organisations is increasing. This is in response to increasing demand for HBOT from people whose disorders are not included on the list of those for which the NHS provides HBOT because there is sparse clinical evidence to support the use of HBOT in many of these other conditions.

HBOT poses safety risks if chambers are incorrectly operated. Excessive oxygen levels will increase the risk of fire and strict control is needed to minimise the presence of flammable materials. There have been isolated fire and explosion incidents worldwide, both in single occupancy chambers in private use and multiplace chambers under medical supervision. In addition, breathing oxygen under pressure can have ill effects. The consensus of opinion among experts is that specific regulation of the treatment is welcomed.

The NCSC will therefore regulate hyperbaric chambers used for therapeutic purposes.

Hyperbaric facilities vary in capacity. A multiplace chamber can accommodate more than one patient with an attendant inside the chamber. A monoplace chamber accommodates one patient only, with the attendant outside the chamber.

Chambers regulated by the NCSC will be classified as Type 1, 2 or 3 depending on the levels of critical care management provided, as defined in the Department of Health's document *Comprehensive Critical Care*:

- Type 1 chambers – these are able to accept patients who need level 2 or above critical care.

- Type 2 chambers – these are unable to accept patients who need level 2 or above critical care at the time of referral, or who are thought likely to deteriorate to those levels during hyperbaric treatment.

- Type 3 chambers – those chambers used only for the treatment of patients with neurological disorders for which NHS hyperbaric treatment is not clinically indicated, eg multiple sclerosis or cerebral palsy.

Certain hyperbaric chambers will be exempted in the regulations from registering with the NCSC. These include those run by the armed forces for the treatment of their own staff; and where the primary purpose of the chamber is pursuant to regulation 6(3)(b) of the Diving at Work Regulations 1997 or regulation 8 or 12 of the Work in Compressed Air Regulations 1996. These chambers will not be available for the general public.

See also, in particular, regulation 3 of the Private and Voluntary Health Care Regulations.

In Vitro Fertilisation (standards P12 to P16)

The attached regulations and standards reflect the particular interests the NCSC will have in regulating establishments where assisted conception services take place, as opposed to the licensing role that the Human Fertilisation and Embryology Authority (HFEA) has.

The HFEA is a non-departmental public body accountable to the Secretary of State for Health. It was set up in August 1991 by the Human Fertilisation and Embryology Act 1990. The HFEA's creation reflected public and professional concern about the potential future of human embryo research and infertility treatments, and a widespread desire for statutory regulation of this highly sensitive area. The HFEA's principal tasks are to licence and monitor those clinics that carry out in vitro fertilisation (IVF), donor insemination and human embryo research. HFEA also regulates the storage of gametes (sperm and eggs) and embryos.

The NCSC will supplement the work of the HFEA by concentrating on aspects of fertility treatment that are outside the remit of the HFEA.

See also, in particular, regulation 3 of the Private and Voluntary Health Care Regulations.

Class 3B and 4 Lasers and/or Intense Pulsed Light Sources

Procedures for Use of Lasers and Intense Pulsed Lights

OUTCOME

Patients receive treatment using lasers and intense pulsed lights from competent operators and in accordance with appropriate procedures.

STANDARD P1

P1.1   **A protocol produced by an expert medical or dental practitioner is followed which sets out the necessary pre-treatment checks and tests, the manner in which the procedure is to be applied, the acceptable variations in the settings used, and when to abort a treatment. In particular, the protocol addresses:**

- contraindications;
- technique;
- pre-treatment tests;
- post-treatment care;
- recognition of treatment-related problems;
- procedure if anything goes wrong with treatment;
- permitted variation on machine variables;
- procedure in the event of equipment failure.

P1.2   The protocol is supported by written procedures for the use of devices, including when they are being used on a trial or demonstration basis, and these cover:

- the potential hazards associated with lasers and/or intense lights;
- controlled and safe access;
- authorised users' responsibilities;
- methods of safe working;
- safety checks;
- normal operating procedures;
- personal protective equipment;
- prevention of use by unauthorised persons; and
- adverse incident procedures.

P1.3   There is a register of persons authorised to use lasers and intense lights. Authorised users sign to indicate that they accept and understand the procedures drawn up for the use of lasers and intense lights in the registered establishment (the Local Rules).

P1.4 Laser and intense light users have access to safety advice from a certificated laser protection adviser.

P1.5 A person with overall on-site responsibility for lasers and intense lights is appointed.

P1.6 Records are maintained every time the laser or intense light is operated, including:
- the name of the person treated;
- the date;
- the operator;
- the treatment given; and
- any accidents or adverse effects.

Training for Staff using Lasers and Intense Pulsed Lights

OUTCOME
Patients receive treatment from appropriately trained operators.

STANDARD P2

P2.1 All laser and intense pulsed light users have training, which is recorded and covers the following:
- **characteristic features of light from lasers and intense pulsed light sources;**
- **hazards from device malfunction;**
- **equipment management;**
- **effects of light on the eye, skin and body tissues;**
- **safety management, including Local Rules and controlled areas;**
- **minimising risks;**
- **action to be taken in the event of an adverse incident.**

P2.2 All staff using lasers and intense pulsed lights have regular update training, both planned and in reaction to relevant technological and medical developments.

P2.3 All operators of lasers and intense pulsed light sources use them only for treatments for which they have been trained and, where appropriate, hold qualifications

Safe Operation of Lasers and Intense Pulsed Lights

OUTCOME

The environment in which lasers and intense pulsed lights are used is safe.

STANDARD P3

P3.1 **The area around working lasers and intense pulsed light sources is controlled to protect other persons while treatment is in progress. The controlled area is clearly defined and not used for other purposes, or as access to areas, when treatment is being carried out.**

P3.2 While the equipment is being operated, the authorised user is responsible for the safety of all persons in the controlled area. No other laser or intense pulsed light source is in use in the same controlled area at the same time.

P3.3 All lasers and intense pulsed light sources have labels identifying them, their wavelength or range of wavelengths, and maximum output power of radiation emitted.

P3.4 In establishments with class 4 lasers, warning signs as specified in EN 60825-1 are displayed on the equipment and on the outside of doors to the controlled area.

P3.5 Protective eyewear is worn by everyone within the controlled area whenever there is a risk of exposure to hazardous levels of laser or intense pulsed light radiation.

P3.6 Operators ensure patient safety by:

- checking with patients if they have any medical condition or treatment for which laser or intense pulsed light treatment would be a contraindication;
- where appropriate, covering the skin outside the area being treated;
- where appropriate, checking the skin type and pigmentation prior to treatment.

P3.7 For all lasers and intense pulsed light sources with a key switch, formal arrangements exist for the safe custody of the key, separate from the equipment. Only authorised users have access to the key. The key is not left unattended with the equipment.

P3.8 Lasers and intense pulsed light sources are regularly serviced and maintained to ensure they are operating within their design specification. A record of servicing and repairs is kept.

Dialysis

Arrangements for Dialysis

> **OUTCOME**
>
> Patients undergo dialysis in accordance with safe and appropriate procedures.

STANDARD P4

P4.1   **There are written criteria for the selection and assessment of patients undergoing dialysis.**

P4.2   The criteria and processes for the selection of suitable patients are monitored.

P4.3   Local protocols for the management of patients, including standards of care to be achieved, are developed and agreed locally by all professionals, based on national guidelines.

P4.4   Where patients are being treated outside hospital, there are explicit arrangements in place for rapid transfer to specialist hospital facilities for unforeseen complications in patients on dialysis.

P4.5   These arrangements are clearly communicated to staff and regularly audited and reviewed.

Facilities for Dialysis

> **OUTCOME**
>
> The environment in which dialysis is undertaken is safe and appropriate.

STANDARD P5

P5.1   **There is space around each bed/chair to allow nursing practice to take place and reduce the risk of cross-infection.**

P5.2   There is screening of each bed space to ensure privacy for patients.

P5.3   There is dirty utility area, separate from clean areas, for safe disposal of clinical waste.

P5.4   There is safe storage for chemical substances, all of which are fully labelled.

P5.5   There are hand washing facilities for staff in the clinical area.

P5.6   If hepatitis B infected patients are treated, isolation facilities are available and used.

P5.7 Department of Health guidelines on the prevention of blood-borne virus infection in renal dialysis units are followed.

P5.8 Where haemodialysis is given, the specific standards for water quality for haemodialysis, set out in the latest version of the Renal Association's standards document, Treatment for adult patients with renal failure, and the appropriate test schedules therein, are complied with.

Staffing for Dialysis

OUTCOME

Patients receive dialysis from staff with the relevant expertise.

STANDARD P6

P6.1 **Supervision of nursing care is undertaken by a registered nurse with the relevant English National Board (ENB) certificates (ENB 136 or ENB 134).**

P6.2 All staff who come into contact with patients are offered vaccination against Hepatitis B.

Hyperbaric Oxygen Treatment

Arrangements for Hyperbaric Oxygen Treatment in Type 1, 2 and 3 Chambers

OUTCOME

Patients receive hyperbaric treatment safely and in accordance with appropriate procedures.

STANDARD P7

P7.1 **Recommendations in appropriate guidance, for example those of the British Hyperbaric Association, are complied with.**

P7.2 The hyperbaric unit works to a set of STANDARD operating procedures (the Local Rules), which are clearly set out, available to and complied with by all staff.

P7.3 The written operating procedures cover:

- the potential hazards associated with hyperbaric chambers;
- methods of safe working;
- safety checks;

- normal operating procedures;
- personal protective equipment;
- adverse incident procedures.

P7.4   Personnel involved with providing hyperbaric treatments are trained and assessed as being competent in the following:

- equipment management;
- safety management;
- minimising risks;
- basic resuscitation skills;
- action to be taken in the event of an adverse incident.

P7.5   All staff involved in the provision of hyperbaric treatment have regular update training on the techniques and equipment used.

P7.6   There is equipment available to initiate resuscitation outside of the chamber.

Staff Qualifications and Training for Type 1 and 2 Chambers

OUTCOME

Patients receive treatment in hyperbaric chambers from competent operators.

STANDARD P8

P8.1   The hyperbaric unit operates under the clinical responsibility of a medical director who is a medical practitioner and possesses clinical experience in hyperbaric and diving medicine.

P8.2   The medical director ensures that the theoretical and practical training requirements of staff are met and that regular refresher courses are undertaken.

P8.3   The nursing and technical staff should hold appropriate qualifications eg CHRN, CHT or equivalent.

P8.4   When children under 12 years old are treated, a qualified children's nurse (registered sick children's nurse, RSCN, or registered nurse child branch certificated) accompanies the patient at all times, with the exception of a) attendance inside the hyperbaric chamber, if not appropriate, or b) where delay of treatment until could affect outcome.

P8.5   If the unit treats children there are formal links with a paediatrician to provide advice to the unit.

Facilities for Treatment in Type 1 and 2 Chambers

OUTCOME

Patients receive hyperbaric oxygen treatment in a safe environment.

STANDARD P9

P9.1   **The unit holds the range of equipment needed for establishing and maintaining an airway, including suction equipment and a defibrillator, and a range of appropriate drugs.**

P9.2   Clinical equipment available for use both inside and outside of the chamber includes indirect blood pressure equipment, stethoscope, auroscope/ophthalmoscope, thermometer and equipment for neurological assessment.

P9.3   Equipment for urinary catheterisation, intravenous cannulation, and pneumothorax drainage is also available.

P9.4   Multiplace chambers must have at least two compartments (i.e. an airlock) to allow access and egress of health care professionals and equipment while maintaining pressure.

Patient Care in Type 1 and 2 Chambers

OUTCOME

Appropriate arrangements for patient care are in place.

STANDARD P10

P10.1   **The initial referral is a key point in treatment of patients, and all relevant information is recorded in a standard format.**

P10.2   The clinical status of a patient is clearly established by the duty medical officer before a referral is accepted, and the means of transfer, along with an estimated time of arrival, is agreed.

P10.3   Wherever possible, the transfer arrangements after treatment, such as return to hospital, an intensive care unit or home, are agreed at the time of referral.

P10.4   The unit assesses the patient medically before treatment starts.

Critical Care in Type 1 Chambers

OUTCOME

Patients are assured that where level 2 or level 3 critical care is provided, as appropriate, within the hyperbaric chamber, it is done so effectively.

STANDARD P11

P11.1   **Patients requiring level 2 or 3 critical care receive it either at the hyperbaric chamber, or are transferred immediately and quickly to the nearest facility that provides it.**

P11.2   Where level 2 or 3 critical care is provided within the hyperbaric chamber:

- there is a written operational policy and protocols for critical care management in the chamber;

- staff are briefed on the policy and protocols so that they are aware of what they should do in specific circumstances;

- the duty medical officer is experienced to specialist registrar standards in either anaesthetics or intensive care medicine.

P11.3   Monitoring equipment available for both inside and outside the chamber includes ECG, pulse oximetry, capnography, invasive blood pressure equipment, mechanical ventilator (hyperbaric compatible), and syringe drivers.

P11.4   Arrangements are in place to transfer patients to critical care facilities where necessary, and are agreed in advance with the hospital most likely to receive such patients.

P11.5   The unit provides equipment to enable the safe transfer of patients to critical care facilities.

P11.6   The unit has arrangements with a local hospital for radiographic and laboratory investigations.

In Vitro Fertilisation

Qualifications and Training of Staff

OUTCOME

Fertility treatment is provided by appropriately skilled and competent staff.

STANDARD P12

P12.1 There is a lead consultant responsible for the delivery of the clinical services provided who is a member of the Royal College of Obstetricians and Gynaecologists and on the relevant specialist register of the General Medical Council.

P12.2 The person in charge of the embryology/seminology laboratory is qualified with a degree in medical or biological science, or an HND in a discipline appropriate to the work being undertaken, or a professional qualification in medical laboratory work.

P12.3 All health care professionals undertaking assisted conception techniques have undergone training and supervised practice in these techniques and have certification or a signed statement to this effect.

P12.4 All staff members of the service receive training and regular up-dates on the legal framework within which the assisted conception services are working.

P12.5 All members of staff in contact with patients are routinely tested for chicken pox and rubella.

Management of Patients

OUTCOME

Patients receive appropriate treatment.

STANDARD P13

P13.1 Local protocols for the management of patients are developed and agreed by all professionals.

P13.2 Local protocols for the prevention and management of ovarian hyperstimulation syndrome are available in all premises carrying out ovulation induction and assisted conception.

P13.3 All deaths, including from ovarian hyperstimulation, are reported to the Confidential Enquiry into Maternal Deaths (CEMD) whether or not the woman had a positive pregnancy test.

P13.4   There are protocols for health care professionals on the value of semen cryostorage in cases where men are undergoing medical treatment likely to make them infertile, so the situation is dealt with quickly and effectively.

P13.5   There are written protocols for the close monitoring of patients, in order to avoid unnecessary complications, including multiple pregnancy.

P13.6   Written protocols set out that no more than, either, two eggs or two embryos are placed in a woman in any one cycle, regardless of the procedure used, and this is recorded in clinical notes and monitored. In exceptional circumstances three eggs/embryos may be placed but there must be documentation in line with the HFEA's Code of Practice explaining why it is necessary.

Patient Information and Decision Making

OUTCOME

Patients are effectively involved in making decisions about treatment.

STANDARD P14

P14.1   **The appropriateness of the treatment is fully considered with all people seeking treatment, including advice on the chance of a live birth following treatment.**

P14.2   In each individual case the decision to recommend treatment is based on the likelihood that a pregnancy will not occur without treatment.

P14.3   Prior to consideration of treatment for unexplained infertility, consideration is given to the likelihood of treatment-independent pregnancy, depending on the woman's age, the duration of infertility and the previous pregnancy history.

P14.4   There is written information for patients setting out the factors that will be taken into consideration before treatment can be confirmed.

P14.5   Prior to patients giving consent to treatment, they are given specific information about:

- the risks associated with multiple pregnancy and birth; and
- the risk of ovarian hyperstimulation syndrome.

P14.6   There is written information for people seeking treatment and those considering donation on the safeguarding of confidentiality.

P14.7   There is written information for patients on the assisted conception treatments and techniques provided by the service, which includes the possible risks and side effects of treatments and the verified live birth rate for the service.

P14.8   All publicity material conforms to the general principles in the guidelines of the GMC and the Code of Professional Conduct of the Nurses and Midwives Council.

Counselling for Patients

OUTCOME

Patients make informed decisions about treatment and are supported during it.

STANDARD P15

P15.1 **All patients are offered the opportunity for independent counselling on the implications of treatment before consent to treatment is given.**

P15.2 Counselling is made available throughout all stages of infertility investigations and treatment, and after the treatment process is complete. Where pregnancy occurs as a result of treatment, the offer of further counselling is also considered.

P15.3 Whenever genetic tests are proposed, written and oral information is provided and counselling is offered by an appropriately trained person.

P15.4 There is information for patients on national counselling organisations which can provide ongoing therapeutic counselling services.

Facilities for Assisted Conception Services

OUTCOME

The facilities are appropriate for fertility treatment.

STANDARD P16

P16.1 **The service facilities and layout are designed to ensure that the need for privacy of donors and people seeking treatment is met.**

P16.2 The room used for egg collection for in vitro fertilisation is close to the laboratory where fertilisation is to take place.

P16.3 There is a dedicated room for the production of semen specimens.

P16.4 There is secure, atmospheric and temperature controlled storage for gametes/embryos and reagents.

P16.5 There are written procedures for the indelible labelling of material from individual patients to ensure the unique identification of a patient's material and records at all stages of treatment.

P16.6 Gametes and embryos are stored in a secure designated area with access by authorised personnel only.

15

Private Doctors

Introduction to Standards PD1 to PD12

These standards cover a variety of services that are provided by private medical practitioners. They apply to:

- private walk-in medical centres, where services are provided by a medical practitioner;
- exclusively private medical practitioners (ie those who do no NHS work at all); and
- agencies that provide medical practitioners to private patients, for example in the patients own home, hotel or workplace.

Independent Clinics

Exclusively private medical practitioners and private walk-in medical centres will be brought within regulation for the first time. Exclusively private medical practitioners include a range of doctors such as private GPs, consultants and psychiatrists who fall outside the NHS clinical governance framework. It is therefore essential that they are regulated to help ensure the delivery of quality care to their patients.

The NCSC's interest is in independent health care services to which the general public has access. In line with this, regulation does *not* extend to private medical practitioners to whom the general public does not have access, for instance those doctors whose work solely comprises the provision of occupational health services for the employees of an organisation, or doctors who solely provide services for insurance companies or Government Departments.

Many of the elements necessary to provide quality assurance in a private medical practitioner's premises or in a private walk-in medical centre are already covered in the core standards. These additional service-specific standards build on the core standards to reflect the nature of the provision of treatment in such premises, such as consultations, health assessments, screening and vaccinations.

There has been concern about whether a patient's GP should be informed of the treatment provided in a walk-in medical centre. This is of course confidential but it is important that the patient should have the opportunity to have this information passed to his/her GP if they so wish. Therefore, the standards require the registered person to have a policy in place for seeking the person's consent or refusal to send the details of the treatment to his/her GP and, if the person agrees, the timescale in which this will be carried out.

Independent Medical Agencies

'Independent medical agencies' brings within the regulatory framework medical practitioners who provide treatment to private patients but who do not operate from establishments that could be registered. This service was highlighted in an article in *Health Which* in August 1999. The article described these agencies as organisations that provide medical practitioners who are at the end of a phone and who can visit a patient in their own home or elsewhere within a short period of time. The patient might call them because their own doctor is unable to attend a house-call or where a person is from out of town and staying in a hotel. The standards aim to provide patients with quality assurance about such doctors.

See also, in particular, regulations 4, 5, 48 and 49 of the Private and Voluntary Health Care Regulations.

Independent Clinics

Arrangements for Provision of Treatment

OUTCOME

Patients are assured that appropriate arrangements for all aspects of their treatment are in place.

STANDARD PD1

PD1.1 The medical history of the patient is ascertained before any treatment is provided.

PD1.2 Patients are advised of the expected fee for the proposed treatment or consultation in advance of treatment being initiated.

PD1.3 Where potentially serious conditions or those of clinical significance are identified there are referral systems in place to guarantee appropriate clinical follow-up.

PD1.4 Private areas offering auditory privacy are provided for consultations.

Management of Patients

OUTCOME

Patients with chronic diseases receive the appropriate level of care and advice on how to control their disease.

STANDARD PD2

PD2.1 **There are protocols adopted for the management of chronic diseases which are used to guide the care provided for illnesses such as:**

- **asthma;**
- **diabetes;**
- **hypertension;**
- **coronary heart disease.**

PD2.2 Patients with chronic diseases are offered appropriate education and advice to enable them to be both involved in their care and to control their disease and reduce associated risk factors.

Minor Surgery

OUTCOME

Minor surgery takes place safely.

STANDARD PD3

PD3.1 **Where minor surgery takes place it does so in a suitably designed and maintained room, the walls and floor of which are finished in a material that keeps it free from infection.**

PD3.2 A couch or theatre table is provided on which the minor surgery takes place.

PD3.3 All health care professionals are trained in basic resuscitation.

PD3.4 Resuscitation equipment is available for use and is checked at least weekly.

PD3.5 There are written procedures for dealing with emergencies, including arrangements for transfers to hospital.

Midwifery and Antenatal Care

OUTCOME

Midwifery and antenatal care are provided effectively.

STANDARD PD4

PD4.1 **Patients who choose to be cared for solely by a midwifery practitioner are assessed to ascertain if there are likely to be any complications at a later stage and these are explained to them. A clear evidence-based referral protocol to obstetric consultant care for women at recognised risk of possible complications is in place.**

PD4.2 Antenatal care and screening tests and quality standards comply, as a minimum, with the standards detailed in the antenatal screening programme of the National Screening Committee and with guidelines from the National Institute of Clinical Excellence (NICE) about antenatal care.

Prescribing of Medication

OUTCOME

Medication is prescribed safely and effectively.

STANDARD PD5

PD5.1 **There are policies in place for the effective prescribing of medication, which are in line with published evidence.**

PD5.2 When treating patients for drug misuse the Department of Health *Guidelines on Drug Misuse and Dependence – Guidelines on Clinical Management* are followed.

PD5.3 Patients are given information about the medications that are prescribed to them including how to take them, the benefits and possible side effects.

PD5.4 Arrangements for repeat prescribing ensure that all patients receiving regular medications are reviewed at intervals, and at least annually.

PD5.5 The prescribing of antidepressants and benzodiazepines are monitored regularly in the light of evidence-based guidelines.

PD5.6 There is a record of the drugs stored in the establishment.

Pathology Services

OUTCOME

Patients are assured that effective pathology services are in place.

STANDARD PD6

PD6.1 **There are written procedures for the accurate recording and labelling of all specimens.**

PD6.2 Specimens are stored at the appropriate temperature.

PD6.3 There is a written agreement with a laboratory for the provision of pathology services.

PD6.4 There are written procedures for the transfer and transportation of specimens, including arrangements for the protection of those handling such items in transit.

Contacting Practitioners and Out-of-Hours Services

OUTCOME

Patients are able to contact private doctors.

STANDARD PD7

PD7.1 **Contact information is available, including all telephone numbers and times of regular sessions worked elsewhere, to ensure that the medical practitioner can be contacted promptly in the case of emergency.**

PD7.2 Private GPs provide an out-of-hours service that ensures:

- patients are able to contact the GP out-of-hours, normally by making no more than two telephone calls to do so;

- that a medical practitioner deputising for the GP is properly inducted and is made aware of their responsibilities under the Care Standards Act 2000;

- that an effective system is in place for transferring and acting on information about patients seen by other medical practitioners during out-of-hours.

Information to GPs

OUTCOME

Patients are offered the opportunity to give or refuse consent for information on their treatment to be passed to their normal GP.

STANDARD PD8

PD8.1 **The registered person for a private walk-in medical centre ensures that there is a policy in place for asking the patient to formally give or refuse consent to inform their normal GP of any treatment or medication provided.**

PD8.2 If the patient gives consent, details are sent to the patient's GP within a locally agreed timescale, but which is no more than 4 weeks.

PD8.3 If the patient does not give consent for details to be sent to his/her GP, a summary of the treatment provided is given direct to the patient so that he/she has it for future reference, to pass on to the GP.

Independent Medical Agencies

Arrangements for Provision of Treatment

OUTCOME

Patients are assured that appropriate arrangements for all aspects of their treatment are in place.

STANDARD PD9

PD9.1 **The medical history of the patient is ascertained before any treatment is provided.**

PD9.2 Patients are advised of the expected fee for the proposed treatment or consultation in advance of treatment being initiated.

PD9.3 Where potentially serious conditions or those of clinical significance are identified there are referral systems in place to guarantee appropriate clinical follow-up.

Prescribing of Medication

OUTCOME

Medication is prescribed safely and effectively.

STANDARD PD10

PD10.1 There are policies in place for the effective prescribing of medication, which are in line with published evidence.

PD10.2 When treating patients for drug misuse the Department of Health *Guidelines on Drug Misuse and Dependence – Guidelines on Clinical Management* are followed.

PD10.3 Patients are given information about the medications that are prescribed to them including how to take them, the benefits and possible side effects.

PD10.4 The prescribing of antidepressants and benzodiazepines are monitored regularly in the light of evidence-based guidelines.

PD10.5 There is a record of the drugs stored by the agency.

Pathology Services

OUTCOME

Patients are assured that effective pathology services are in place.

STANDARD PD11

PD11.1 There are written procedures for the accurate recording and labelling of all specimens.

PD11.2 Specimens are stored at the appropriate temperature.

PD11.3 There is a written agreement with a laboratory for the provision of pathology services.

PD11.4 There are written procedures for the transfer and transportation of specimens, including arrangements for the protection of those handling such items in transit.

Information to GPs

OUTCOME

Patients are offered the opportunity to give or refuse consent for information on their treatment to be passed to their normal GP.

STANDARD PD12

PD12.1 The registered person ensures that there is a policy in place for asking the patient to formally give, or refuse, consent to inform their normal GP of any treatment or medication provided.

PD12.2 If the patient gives consent, details are sent to the patient's GP within a locally agreed timescale, but which is no more than 4 weeks.

PD12.3 If the patient does not give consent for details to be sent to his/her GP, a summary of the treatment provided is given direct to the patient so that he/she has it for future reference, to pass on to the GP.

Appendices

Categories and Numbers of Independent Health Care Providers

Establishments/Agencies	Estimated number
Independent Hospitals	
1. Acute hospitals (including day surgery hospitals)	195
2. Establishments where Mental Health treatment mainly takes place	195
3. Hospices	160
4. Maternity hospitals	2
5. Termination of pregnancy establishments	76
6. Establishments where treatment is provided using certain prescribed techniques and technologies:	
a) (i) Class 3b and 4c laser/intense light source users	1,048
(ii) Other users of intense light sources	230
b) Dialysis	12
c) Endoscopy	2
d) Hyperbaric chambers	42
e) In vitro fertilisation	46
Independent Clinics	
7. Private doctors:	
a) Walk-in medical-centres	15
b) Exclusively private doctors	200
Independent Medical Agencies	
8. Private call out doctors	9
TOTAL	**2,232**

Sources

1 DoH Survey of Health & Local Authority Registration & Inspection Units 1999/2000

2 DoH Survey of Health & Local Authority Registration & Inspection Units 1999/2000 (Laing's Healthcare Market Review 2000/01 lists 79 independent acute psychiatric hospitals in England)

3 DoH Survey of Health & Local Authority Registration & Inspection Units 1999/2000

4 DoH Estimate (NB figures exclude those maternity hospitals that are also acute hospitals)

5 DoH Sexual Health Branch

6 a) (i) DoH Survey Estimate
      (ii) Industry Estimate (NB this figure is based on industry estimates and may include UK-wide clinics rather than those just in England)

   b) National Kidney Federation Website (NB this figure does not include dialysis within acute hospitals)

   c) & e) DoH Policy Estimate

   d) Federation of Multiple Sclerosis Therapy Centres Booklet 1998

7 a) & b) Laing's Healthcare Market Review 2000/01 and internet information

8 Health Which Article, August 1999

Glossary of Terms

Accident

Any unexpected or unforeseen occurrence, especially one that results in injury or damage.

Accident report

A written report of an accident. The format of the report is laid down in health and safety legislation.

Accountability

The state of being answerable for one's decisions and actions. Accountability cannot be delegated.

Audit

The process of setting or adopting standards and measuring performance against those standards with the aim of identifying both good and bad practice and implementing changes to achieve unmet standards.

Adolescents

Young people in the process of moving from childhood to adulthood. Adolescents may have special needs as patients/users.

Adverse clinical incident

An incident, accident or occurrence, relating to clinical systems or procedures which results in harm, or an injury, or near miss to a patient/user or member of staff.

Advocate

An individual who acts independently on behalf of, and in the interests of, patients/users who may feel unable to represent themselves in their contacts with a health care or other facility.

Aim

Overall purpose or goal of a department or service.

Annual report

A report, written annually, which details progress over the last year and plans for the following year, which includes financial and activity statements.

Care plan

A document which details the care and treatment that a patient/user receives and identifies who delivers the care an treatment. This term covers the term 'individual plan' (see also health record).

Care programme approach (CPA)

The individual packages of care (care programmes), developed in conjunction with social services, for all patients accepted by the specialist psychiatric services. Care programmes may range from 'minimal' single worker assessment and monitoring, for individuals with less severe mental health and social needs, to complex and multi professional assessments and treatment.

Carer

A person who may be paid or unpaid, who regularly helps another person, often a relative or friend with domestic, physical, emotional or personal care as a result of illness or disability. This term incorporates spouses, partners, parents, guardians, paid carers, other relatives, and voluntary carers who are not health professionals.

Checklist

A means of recording observations relating to fixed criteria, used to check compliance with agreed procedures or standards.

Clinical governance

A framework through which NHS organisations are accountable for continuously improving the quality of their services and safeguarding high standards of care by creating an environment in which excellence in clinical care will flourish.

Clinical responsibilities

Range of activities for which a clinician is accountable.

Consultant

Medical Practitioner who works independently without supervision.

Continuing education

Activities which provide education and training to staff. These may be used to prepare for specialisation or career development as well as facilitating personal development.

Contract/agreement

The document agreed between providers of health care and the purchasers of health care detailing activity, financial and quality levels to be achieved.

COSHH

Acronym for the control of substances hazards to health legislation.

Criterion

A measurable component of performance. A number of criteria need to be met to achieve the desired standards.

Critical care – Level 1

Patients at risk of their condition deteriorating, or those recently relocated from higher levels of care, whose needs can be met on an acute ward without additional advice and support from the critical care team.

Critical care – Level 2

Patients requiring more detailed observation or intervention including support for a single failing organ system or post-operative care and those stepping down from higher levels of care.

Critical care – Level 3

Patients requiring advanced respiratory support alone or basic respiratory support together with support of at least two organ systems. This level includes all complex patients requiring support for multi-organ failure.

Duty of care

Duty of health care staff to put the care and safety of the patient/user first in all circumstances.

Errors

Mistakes made by staff in the performance of their duties.

Evaluation

The study of the performance of a service (or element of treatment and care) with the aim of identifying successful and problem areas of activity.

Food hygiene

Taking all measures necessary to ensure the safety and wholesomeness of foodstuffs.

Hazards

The potential to cause harm, including ill-health and injury, damage to property, plant, products or the environment, production losses or increased liabilities.

Health and safety policy

A plan of action for the health, safety and well-being of staff, patients/users, residents and visitors.

Healthcare workers

Any staff who come into direct contact with patients who are receiving treatment, including ancillary staff as well as healthcare professionals.

Health record

The record of all aspects of the patients treatment, otherwise known as the patients notes.

Hospital acquired infection

An infection acquired by a patient/user during their stay in hospital which is unconnected with their reason for admission.

ICD code

International classification of diseases coding system.

Incident

An event or occurrence, especially one which leads to problems. An example of this could be an attack on one person by another within a service.

Induction programme

Learning activities designed to enable newly appointed staff to function effectively in a new position.

Job description

Details of accountability, responsibility, formal lines of communication, principal duties, entitlements and performance review. A guide for an individual in a specific position within an organisation.

Keyworker

A keyworker is the person responsible for co-ordinating the care plan for each individual patient/user, for monitoring its progress and for staying in regular contact with the patient/user and everyone involved. A keyworker can come from a variety of different professional or non-professional backgrounds.

Manual handling

Any transportation of a load by picking up, setting down, pushing, pulling, carrying or moving thereof, by hand or bodily force.

Monitoring

The systematic process of collecting information on clinical and non-clinical performance. Monitoring may be intermittent or continuous. It may also be undertaken in relation to specific incidents of concern or to check key performance areas.

Multiprofessional

A combination of several professions working towards a common aim.

Near miss

An incident, or an incident avoided, which it is realised had the potential to cause harm on injury.

Objective

A specific and measurable statement which set out how overall aims are to be achieved.

Organisation

The term used in this publication to describe the entire organisation, as opposed to the term service, which is used to describe one part of the organisation (see also service).

Organisational chart

A graphical representation of the structure of the organisation including areas of responsibility, relationships and formal lines of communication and accountability.

Outcome

The end result of care and treatment, that is the change in health, functional ability, symptoms or situation of the person, which can be used to measure the effectiveness of care and treatment.

Patient survey

Seeking the views of patients through responses to pre-prepared questions and carried out through interview or self-completion questionnaires.

Personnel

All those who work in the regulated establishment/agency i.e. those with practising privileges as well as staff.

Planning

The process by which the service determines how it will achieve its aims and objectives. This includes identifying the resources which will be needed to meet the aims and objectives.

Policy

An operational statement of intent in a given situation.

Procedure

The steps taken to fulfil a policy.

Professional standards

Professionally agreed levels of performance.

Protocol

The adoption, by all staff, of national or local guidelines to meet local requirements in a specified way.

Quality Assurance (QA)

A generic term to cover the review of the quality of services provided, along with interventions designed to improve that quality through the remedying of deficiencies identified by the review process. The review may include both qualitative and quantitative measurements and may or may not relate to clearly stated standards.

Research and development

The searching out of knowledge and evidence about the relationship between different factors in the provision of services. Research does not require action in response to findings.

Review

The examination of a particular aspect of a service or care setting so that problem areas requiring corrective action can be identified.

Risk management

A systematic approach to the management of risk, to reduce loss of life, financial loss, loss of staff availability, staff and patient/client/user safety, loss of availability of buildings or equipment, or loss of reputation.

Risk management strategy

A written statement of objectives for the management of risk and a plan for meeting those objectives. The strategy should be consistent with the business plan.

Serious untoward incident

An accident or occurrence which results in significant injury to a patient/user, member of staff, carer or visitor.

Skill mix

The balance of skill, qualifications and experience of nursing and other clinical staff employed in a particular area.

Staff

Those employed by the regulated establishment/agency.

Standard

An overall statement of desired performance.

Survey

The collection of views from a sample of people in order to obtain a representative picture of the views of the total population being studied.

Untoward incident

Any incident, accident or occurrence, relating to clinical or non clinical work which could result in an injury or near miss to a patient/user member of staff or visitor.

Valid consent

The legal principle by which a patient/user is informed about the nature, purpose and likely effects of any treatment proposed before being asked to consent to accepting it.

Vital services

These services are essential to the normal operation of the organisation. Examples include electricity, water, medical gases and telecommunications.

Policies, procedures and protocols

Independent health care providers will develop policies, procedures and protocols appropriate to the setting, for the following:

Core Requirements

Arrangements for admission, acceptance transfer and discharge of patients	Reg 9
Arrangements for assessment, diagnosis and treatment of patients	Reg 9
Ensuring patients give consent to treatment	Reg 9
Disclosure of patient information	Reg 9
Ensuring that care is patient-centred, including:	Std C2
Patients consent to examinations	Std C2
Patients consultation about treatment	Std C2
Patients access to health records	Std C2
Patients privacy, dignity, confidentiality	Std C2
Responding to advance directives	Std C2
Prevention of harassment and bullying	Std C2
Monitoring quality of clinical treatment and care	Std C4
Human resources	Reg 9
Human resources	Std C9
Granting practising privileges	Std C10
Child protection	Std C13
Handling complaints	Reg 23
Complaints process	Std C14
Fitness of the premises	Reg 9
Monitoring the suitability of facilities and equipment	Reg 9
Workers concerns	Std C16
Maintenance of the premises	Std C17
Risk Management	Reg 9
Informing the NCSC of staff suspensions on clinical grounds	Std C20
Risk management	Std C20
Handling waste	Std C21
Interruption of medical gas lines	Std C21
Moving and handing of patients	Std C21
Medicines management	Std C21
Infection control	Std C25

Resuscitation	Std C27
Records and information management	Reg 9
Information provision	Reg 9
Research	Std C32

Service-Specific Requirements

Acute hospitals

Resuscitation	Reg 32
Out of hours cover for allied health professionals	Std A7
Infection control	Std A9
Decontamination	Std A11
Manual cleaning	Std A11
Pain management for children	Std A18
Transfer of children	Std A19
Procedures for surgery	Std A20–21
Use of cosmetic surgery equipment	Std A26
Day surgery	Std 27
Conduct of transplantation (including donor organs/Xenotransplantation)	Std A28
Critical care	Std A29
Critical care: post operative management	Std A30
Radiology	Std A31
Use of patients own drugs	Std A34
Medication, including self-medication	Std A36
Medical gas cylinders	Std A39
Pathology services	Std A41–42
Chemotherapy	Std A44
Radiotherapy	Std A45

Mental Health Establishments

Safety of the patient and others	Reg 44
Management of disturbed behaviour	Reg 45
Patients receiving visitors	Reg 46
The Mental Health National Service Framework	Std M1
Communication between staff re patient treatment	Std M2
Patient confidentiality	Std M3
Risk management	Std M7
Suicide prevention	Std M8
Infection control	Std M9
Resuscitation	Std M10
The Care Programme Approach	Std M11
Voluntary admission	Std M12
Patients with developmental disabilities	Std M15

Electro-convulsive therapy	Std M16
Administration of medicines	Std M17–18
Treatment for addictions	Std M19
Transfer of patients	Std M20
Patient discharge	Std M21
Arrangements for visiting	Std M24
Working with carers and family members	Std M25
Restrictions and security for patients	Std M29
Levels of observation	Std M30
Managing disturbed behaviour	Std M31
Managing serious/untoward incidents	Std M32
Unexpected patient death	Std M33
Patients absconding	Std M34
Patient restraint and physical interventions	Std M35
Safeguarding children	Std M36
Functions of hospital managers	Std M41
Assessment, care, treatment and discharge of detained patients	Std M41
The rights of patients under the Mental Health Act	Std M42
Seclusion of patients	Std M43
Leave for detained patients	Std M44
Staff training on the Mental Health Act	Std M47

Hospices

Infection control	Std H6
Resuscitation	Std H7
Use of patients own drugs	Std H9
Ordering, storage, use and disposal of medicines	Std H9
Medication including self-medication	Std H11
Medical gas cylinders	Std H12

Maternity Hospitals

Infection control	Std MC2
Use of Anti-D	Std MC4
Referral to obstetric consultant care	Std MC5
Antenatal and post-natal wards and the delivery suite	Std MC6
Maternal deaths and still-births	Std MC7
Handling common problems faced by newborn babies	Std MC8

Termination of Pregnancy Establishments

Handing fetal tissue	Reg 41
Respect for fetal tissue	Std TP4
Transfer of patients to hospital	Std TP5

Prescribed Techniques and Technologies

Use of lasers and intense lights	Std P1
Arrangements for dialysis	Std P4
Critical care in type1 chambers	Std P11
Monitoring of patients	Std P13
IVF-labelling	Std P16

Private Doctors (independent clinics)

Emergency procedures re minor surgery	Std PD3
Prescribing and medication	Std PD5
Pathology services	Std PD6
Informing the patient's GP	Std PD8

Private Doctors (independent medical agencies)

Prescribing and medication	Std PD10
Pathology services	Std PD11
Informing the patient's GP	Std PD12

Bibliography

Acute Hospitals

Clinical Pathology Accreditation (2000) *Standards for the Medical Laboratory.* CPA(UK) Ltd. Sheffield.

Department of Health (2000) Resuscitation Policy (HSC2000/028). Department of Health. London.

Department of Health (1991) *Local Research Ethics Committees.* Department of Health. London.

Department of Health (2000) *The NHS Cancer Plan.* Department of Health. London.

Department of Health (2000) *Comprehensive Critical Care Report.* Department of Health. London.

Department of Health (2000) *Coronary Heart Disease National Service Framework.* Department of Health. London.

The Health Quality Service (1999) *The Health Quality Service Accreditation Programme.* HQS. London.

Independent Health Care Association (2001) *Guidance on the Care of Children Receiving Care in Independent Sector Acute Hospitals.* AIH. London.

National Association of Health Authorities and Trusts (1993) *Independent Acute Hospitals & Services – Supplement to the Handbook on Registration and Inspection of Nursing Homes.* NAHAT.

NHS Executive (1999) *Controls Assurance Standard Infection Control.* Department of Health. London.

NHS Executive (2001) *Controls Assurance Standard Decontamination.* Department of Health. London.

Renal Association (1997) *Treatment of Adult Patients with Renal Failure.* Renal Association/Royal College of Physicians. London.

Renal Association (2000) *United Kingdom Guidelines for Living Donor Kidney Transplantation.* Renal Association. London.

Royal College of Anaesthetists (1999) *Guidelines for the Provision of Anaesthetic Services.* RCA. London.

Royal College of Surgeons of England (2000) *Children's Surgery – A First Class Service*. RCS. London.

Mental Health

Centre for Policy on Ageing (1999) *Standards Matter: a conference report on regulating registered residential and nursing homes*. CPA. London.

Department of Health (1990) *Caring for Quality: guidance on Standards for residential homes for people with a physical disability*. HMSO. London.

Department of Health (1996) *Building Bridges*. Dept of Health. London.

Department of Health (1999) *Safer Services: National Confidential inquiry into Suicide and Homicide by people with a mental illness*. London. Dept of Health.

Department of Health and Welsh Office (1999) *Mental health Act 1983 Code of Practice*. The Stationery Office. London.

Department of Health (1999) *Mental Health National Service Frameworks*, Stationery Office. London.

Dept of Health (2000) *Dignity in mental health units: guidance on mixed sex accommodation for mental health services*. HMSO. London.

European Association for the Treatment of Addictions (1999) *Auditing standards: managing quality in the treatment of addictions*. EATA (UK). Rugby.

Health Advisory Service 2000 (1999) *Standards for Adult Mental Health Services*. Pavilion. Brighton.

Mental Health Act Commission and the Sainsbury Centre for Mental Health (1997) *The National Visit*. The Sainsbury Centre. London.

Mental Health Services of Salford NHS Trust and Northern College of Nursing, Midwifery and Health Studies (1995) *The Spirit of the Act: the philosophy behind the mental health act (1983) and the Code of Practice*. Mental Health Services of Salford NHS Trust and Northern College of Nursing, Midwifery and Health Studies. Salford.

MIND (1996) *Not Just Sticks and Stones*. MIND. London.

MIND (1997) *Raised Voices: African-Caribbean and African users views and experiences of mental health services in England and Wales*. MIND Publications. London.

National Schizophrenia Fellowship (1999) *One in Ten: a report into unnatural deaths of people with schizophrenia 1991–1999*. NSF. London.

Royal College of Psychiatrists (1999) *Improving the care of elderly people with mental health problems*. Gaskell. London.

Royal College of Psychiatry (1998) *Management of Imminent Violence*. The Royal College of Psychiatry. London.

Adult Palliative Care

Department of Health. *A First Class Service – Quality in the New NHS*, 1998.

NHS Executive. HSC 1999/065. *Clinical Governance: Quality in the new NHS,* 1999.

National Council for Hospice and Specialist Palliative Care Services. *Briefing Number 3: The Definition and Measurement of Quality in Palliative Care, 1999.*

NHS Executive. EL(95)51. *A Policy Framework for Commissioning Cancer Services, 1995.*

Department of Health. *National Service Framework for Coronary Heart Disease, 2000.*

NHS Executive. EL(96)85. *A Policy Framework for Commissioning Cancer Services: Palliative Care Services*

NHS Executive. HSC 1998/115. *Palliative Care, 1998.*

NHS Executive. HSC 1999/78 *NHS Performance Assessment Framework, 1999.*

National Council for Hospice and Specialist Palliative Care Services. *Guidelines for Managing Cancer Pain in Adults, 1998.*

National Council for Hospice and Specialist Palliative Care Services. *Changing Gear – Guidelines for Managing the Last Days of Life in Adults, 1997.*

National Council for Hospice and Specialist Palliative Care Services. *Palliative Care 2000: Commissioning through partnership, 1999* (Separate versions for Wales and Northern Ireland are to be published in 2000).

National Council for Hospice and Specialist Palliative Care Services. *Making Palliative Care Better: Quality Improvement, multi-professional audit and standards, 1997.*

Department of Health. *The NHS Cancer Plan. A plan for investment. A plan for reform.* September 2000.

Children's Palliative Care

Association for Children with Life-threatening or Terminal Conditions and their Families (ACT) & Royal College of Paediatrics and Child Health (1997) *A Guide to the Development of Children's Palliative Care Services*, ACT/RCPCH, Bristol/London.

Association for Children with Life-threatening or Terminal Conditions and their Families (ACT) ACTPACK information Children's Hospices, ACT, Bristol.

Association for Children with Life-threatening or Terminal Conditions and their Families (ACT) (1994) *The ACT Charter for Children with Life-threatening Conditions and their Families*, ACT, Bristol.

Baum, Dominica & Woodward (1990) *Listen My Child Has A Lot Of Living To Do – Caring for Children with Life-Threatening Conditions,* Oxford University Press, Oxford.

Department for Culture Media and Sport (2000) *New Opportunities from The Lottery – Proposals for the New Opportunities Fund,* DCMS, London.

NHS Executive (1998) *Evaluation of the Pilot Project Programme for Children with Life Threatening Illnesses,* Department of Health, London.

Other References

Department of Health (1998) *Modernising Social Services: Promoting Independence, Improving Protection, Raising Standards.* London: HMSO.

Department of Health (1999) *The Government's Response to Health Committee's Fifth Report on the Regulation of Private and Other Independent Healthcare.* London: HMSO.

Department of Health (1999) *Regulating Private and Voluntary Healthcare: A Consultation Document.*

Department of Health (1999) *Regulating Private and Voluntary Healthcare: The Way Forward.*

Department of Health (2000) *Regulating Private and Voluntary Healthcare: Developing the Way Forward.*

Department of Health (2000) *The Care Standards Act 2000.* London: HMSO.

Private and Voluntary Health Care Regulations

S T A T U T O R Y   I N S T R U M E N T S

2001 No. 3968

PUBLIC HEALTH, ENGLAND

The Private and Voluntary Health Care (England) Regulations 2001

Made - - - - -	*11th December 2001*
Laid before Parliament	*12th December 2001*
Coming into force - -	*1st April 2002*

ARRANGEMENT OF REGULATIONS

PART I

GENERAL

PART II

REGISTERED PERSONS

[1]

PART III

CONDUCT OF HEALTH CARE ESTABLISHMENTS AND AGENCIES

Chapter 1

Quality of service provision

Chapter 2

Premises

Chapter 3

Management

Chapter 4

Notices to be given to the Commission

PART IV

ADDITIONAL REQUIREMENTS APPLYING TO INDEPENDENT HOSPITALS

Chapter 1

Pathology services, resuscitation and treatment of children in independent hospitals

Chapter 2

Independent hospitals in which certain listed services are provided

[2]

The Secretary of State, in exercise of powers conferred on him by sections 2(4), (7)(f) and (8), 22(1), (2)(a) to (d), (f) to (j), (5)(a) and (7)(a) to (h), (j) and (k), 25(1), 34(1), 35(1) and 118(5) to (7) of the Care Standards Act 2000(**a**) and of all other powers enabling him in that behalf, having consulted such persons as he considers appropriate(**b**), hereby makes the following Regulations:—

(**a**) 2000 c. 14. The powers are exercisable by the appropriate Minister, who is defined in section 121(1), in relation to England, Scotland and Northern Ireland, as the Secretary of State, and in relation to Wales, as the National Assembly for Wales. "Prescribed" and "regulations" are defined in section 121(1) of the Act.

(**b**) *See* section 22(9) of the Care Standards Act 2000 for the requirement to consult.

[3]

PART I

GENERAL

Citation, commencement and extent

1.—(1) These Regulations may be cited as the Private and Voluntary Health Care (England) Regulations 2001 and shall come into force on 1st April 2002.

(2) These Regulations extend to England only.

Interpretation

2.—(1) In these Regulations—

"the Act" means the Care Standards Act 2000;

"agency" means an independent medical agency;

"dentist" means a person registered in the dentists register under the Dentists Act 1984(**a**);

"establishment" means an independent hospital, including an independent hospital in which treatment or nursing (or both) are provided for persons liable to be detained under the Mental Health Act 1983(**b**), or an independent clinic;

"general practitioner" means a medical practitioner who—

(a) provides general medical services within the meaning of Part II of the NHS Act;

(b) performs personal medical services in connection with a pilot scheme under the National Health Service (Primary Care) Act 1997(**c**); or

(c) provides services which correspond to services provided under Part II of the NHS Act, otherwise than in pursuance of that Act;

"health care professional" means a person who is registered as a member of any profession to which section 60(2) of the Health Act 1999(**d**) applies, or who is a clinical psychologist or child psychotherapist, and "health care profession" shall be construed accordingly;

"medical device" has the same meaning as in the Medical Devices Regulations 1994(**e**);

"medical practitioner" means a registered medical practitioner(**f**);

"midwife" means a registered midwife(**g**) who has notified her intention to practise to the local supervisory authority in accordance with any rules made under section 14(1)(b) of the Nurses, Midwives and Health Visitors Act 1997(**h**);

"the NHS Act" means the National Health Service Act 1977(**i**);

"organisation" means a body corporate or any unincorporated association other than a partnership;

"patient", in relation to any establishment or agency, means a person for whom treatment is provided in or for the purposes of the establishment, or for the purposes of the agency;

"patients' guide" means the guide compiled in accordance with regulation 7;

"practising privileges" in relation to a medical practitioner, refers to the grant to a person who is not employed in an independent hospital of permission to practise in that hospital;

"registered manager", in relation to an establishment or agency, means a person who is registered under Part II of the Act as the manager of the establishment or agency;

"registered person", in relation to an establishment or agency, means any person who is the registered provider or the registered manager of the establishment or agency;

"registered provider", in relation to an establishment or agency, means a person who is registered under Part II of the Act as the person carrying on the establishment or agency;

"responsible individual" shall be construed in accordance with regulation 10(2)(b)(i);

(**a**) 1984 c. 24.
(**b**) 1983 c. 20.
(**c**) 1997 c. 46.
(**d**) 1999 c. 8.
(**e**) S.I. 1994/3017.
(**f**) *See* the Interpretation Act 1978 (c. 30), Schedule 1, as amended by the Medical Act 1983 (c. 54), section 56(1), Schedule 5, paragraph 18.
(**g**) *See* the Interpretation Act 1978, Schedule 1. A definition of "registered" in relation to midwives was inserted by the Nurses, Midwives and Health Visitors Act 1979 (c. 36), Schedule 7, paragraph 30.
(**h**) 1997 c. 24.
(**i**) 1977 c. 49.

[4]

"statement of purpose" means the written statement compiled in accordance with regulation 6;

"treatment" includes palliative care and nursing and listed services within the meaning of section 2 of the Act(**a**).

(2) In these Regulations, a reference—

(a) to a numbered regulation or Schedule is to the regulation in, or Schedule to, these Regulations bearing that number;

(b) in a regulation or Schedule to a numbered paragraph, is to the paragraph in that regulation or Schedule bearing that number;

(c) in a paragraph to a lettered or numbered sub-paragraph is to the sub-paragraph in that paragraph bearing that letter or number.

(3) In these Regulations, references to employing a person include employing a person whether under a contract of service or a contract for services, and references to an employee or to a person being employed shall be construed accordingly.

Prescribed techniques or technology and exceptions to the definition of independent hospital

3.—(1) Subject to paragraph (2), for the purposes of section 2 of the Act, "listed services" include treatment using any of the following techniques or technology—

(a) a Class 3B or Class 4 laser product, as defined in Part I of British Standard EN 60825–1 (Radiation safety of laser products and systems)(**b**);

(b) an intense light, being broadband non-coherent light which is filtered to produce a specified range of wavelengths; such filtered radiation being delivered to the body with the aim of causing thermal, mechanical or chemical damage to structures such as hair follicles and skin blemishes while sparing surrounding tissues;

(c) haemodialysis or peritoneal dialysis;

(d) endoscopy;

(e) hyperbaric oxygen therapy, being the administration of pure oxygen through a mask to a patient who is in a sealed chamber which is gradually pressurised with compressed air, except where the primary use of that chamber is—

(i) pursuant to regulation 6(3)(b) of the Diving at Work Regulations 1997(**c**) or regulation 8 or 12 of the Work in Compressed Air Regulations 1996(**d**); or

(ii) otherwise for the treatment of workers in connection with the work which they perform; and

(f) in vitro fertilisation techniques, being treatment services for which a licence may be granted under paragraph 1 of Schedule 2 to the Human Fertilisation and Embryology Act 1990(**e**).

(2) Listed services shall not include treatment using the following techniques or technology—

(a) treatment for the relief of muscular and joint pain using an infra-red heat treatment lamp;

(b) treatment using a Class 3B laser where such treatment is carried out by or under the supervision of a health care professional; and

(c) the use of an apparatus (not being an apparatus falling within paragraph (1)(b)), for acquiring an artificial suntan, consisting of a lamp or lamps emitting ultraviolet rays.

(3) For the purposes of section 2 of the Act, establishments of the following descriptions are excepted from being independent hospitals—

(a) an establishment which is a hospital by virtue of section 2(3)(a)(i) of the Act solely because its main purpose is to provide medical or psychiatric treatment for illness or mental disorder but which provides no overnight beds for patients;

(**a**) *See* section 2(7).
(**b**) Copies of BS EN 60825-1 may be obtained from BSI Customer Services, 389 Chiswick High Road, London W4 4AL.
(**c**) S.I. 1997/2776.
(**d**) S.I. 1996/1656.
(**e**) 1990 c. 37.

[5]

(b) an establishment which is a service hospital within the meaning of section 13(9) of the Armed Forces Act 1981(**a**);

(c) an establishment which is, or forms part of, a prison, remand centre, young offender institution or secure training centre within the meaning of the Prison Act 1952(**b**);

(d) an establishment which is an independent clinic by virtue of regulation 4;

(e) an establishment (not being a health service hospital) which has as its sole or main purpose the provision by a general practitioner of general medical services within the meaning of Part II of the NHS Act or personal medical services in connection with a pilot scheme under the National Health Service (Primary Care) Act 1997; and such an establishment shall not become an independent hospital as a result of the provision of listed services to a patient by such a general practitioner;

(f) the private residence of a patient or patients in which treatment is provided to such patient or patients, but to no-one else;

(g) sports grounds and gymnasia where health professionals provide treatment to persons taking part in sporting activities and events; and

(h) a surgery or consulting room, not being part of a hospital, where a medical practitioner provides medical services solely under arrangements made on behalf of the patients by their employer or another person.

(4) Sub-section (7) of section 2 of the Act shall be modified by adding at the end of paragraph (e) (cosmetic surgery) the following—

"(a) other than—

    (i) ear and body piercing;

    (ii) tattooing;

    (iii) the subcutaneous injection of a substance or substances into the skin for cosmetic purposes; and

    (iv) the removal of hair roots or small blemishes on the skin by the application of heat using an electric current.".

Meaning of independent clinic

4.—(1) For the purposes of section 2(4) of the Act, establishments of the following kinds are prescribed—

(a) a walk-in centre, in which one or more medical practitioners provide services of a kind which, if provided in pursuance of the NHS Act, would be provided as general medical services under Part II of that Act; and

(b) a surgery or consulting room in which a medical practitioner who provides no services in pursuance of the NHS Act provides medical services of any kind (including psychiatric treatment) otherwise than under arrangements made on behalf of the patients by their employer or another person.

(2) Where two or more medical practitioners use different parts of the same premises as a surgery or consulting room, or use the same surgery or consulting room at different times, each of the medical practitioners shall be regarded as carrying on a separate independent clinic unless they are in practice together.

Exception of undertaking from the definition of independent medical agency

5. For the purposes of the Act, any undertaking which consists of the provision of medical services by a medical practitioner solely under arrangements made on behalf of the patients by their employer or another person shall be excepted from being an independent medical agency.

(**a**) 1981 c. 55.

(**b**) 1952 c. 52. Amended by section 170(1) of and paragraphs 11 and 12 of Schedule 15, and Schedule 16, to the Criminal Justice Act 1988 (c. 33); sections 5(2), 18(3) and 168(3) of, and Schedule 11 to, the Criminal Justice and Public Order Act 1994 (c. 33); section 119 of, and paragraph 6 of Schedule 8 to, the Crime and Disorder Act 1998 (c. 37); and section 165(1) of, and paragraph 5 of Schedule 9 to, the Powers of the Criminal Courts (Sentencing) Act 2000 (c. 6). Subsection (1)(a) of section 43 is to be repealed by sections 59 and 75 of, and Schedule 8 to, the Criminal Justice and Court Services Act 2000 (c. 43) on a date to be appointed.

Statement of purpose

6.—(1) The registered person shall compile in relation to the establishment or agency a written statement (in these Regulations referred to as "the statement of purpose") which shall consist of a statement as to the matters listed in Schedule 1.

(2) The registered person shall supply a copy of the statement of purpose to the Commission and shall make the statement available for inspection by every patient and any person acting on behalf of a patient.

(3) Nothing in regulation 15(1) or 25(1) and (2) shall require or authorise the registered person to contravene, or not to comply with—

(a) any other provision of these Regulations; or

(b) the conditions for the time being in force in relation to the registration of the registered person under Part II of the Act.

Patients' guide

7.—(1) The registered person shall produce a written guide to the establishment or agency (in these Regulations referred to as "the patients' guide") which shall consist of—

(a) a summary of the statement of purpose;

(b) the terms and conditions in respect of services to be provided for patients, including as to the amount and method of payment of charges for all aspects of their treatment;

(c) a standard form of contract for the provision of services and facilities by the registered provider to patients;

(d) a summary of the complaints procedure established under regulation 23;

(e) a summary of the results of the consultation conducted in accordance with regulation 17(3);

(f) the address and telephone number of the Commission; and

(g) the most recent inspection report prepared by the Commission or information as to how a copy of that report may be obtained.

(2) The registered person shall supply a copy of the patients' guide to the Commission, and shall make the patients' guide available for inspection by every patient and any person acting on behalf of a patient.

Review of statement of purpose and patients' guide

8. The registered person shall—

(a) keep under review and, where appropriate, revise the statement of purpose and the content of the patients' guide; and

(b) notify the Commission of any such revision.

Policies and procedures

9.—(1) The registered person shall prepare and implement written statements of the policies to be applied and the procedures to be followed in or for the purposes of an establishment in relation to—

(a) the arrangements for admission or acceptance of patients, their transfer to a hospital where required and, in the case of an establishment which admits in-patients, their discharge;

(b) the arrangements for assessment, diagnosis and treatment of patients;

(c) ensuring that the premises used by or for the purposes of an establishment are at all times fit for the purpose for which they are used;

(d) monitoring the quality and suitability of facilities and equipment;

(e) identifying, assessing and managing risks to employees, patients and visitors associated with the operation of the establishment;

(f) the creation, management, handling and storage of records and other information;

(g) the provision of information to patients and others;

(h) the recruitment, induction and retention of employees and their employment conditions;

[7]

(i) the grant and withdrawal of practising privileges to medical practitioners in establishments where such privileges are granted; and

(j) ensuring that, where research is carried out in an establishment, it is carried out with the consent of any patient or patients involved, is appropriate for the establishment concerned and is conducted in accordance with up-to-date and authoritative published guidance on the conduct of research projects.

(2) The registered person shall prepare and implement a written statement of the policies to be applied and the procedures to be followed for the purposes of an agency in relation to—

(a) the arrangements for transfer to a hospital, where required; and

(b) each of the matters specified in sub-paragraphs (b), (f), (g) and (h) of paragraph (1).

(3) The registered person shall prepare and implement written statements of policies to be applied and procedures to be followed in or for the purposes of an establishment, or for the purpose of an agency, which ensure that—

(a) the competence of each patient to consent to treatment is assessed;

(b) in the case of a competent patient, properly informed consent to treatment is obtained;

(c) in the case of a patient who is not competent, he is, so far as practicable, consulted before any treatment proposed for him is administered; and

(d) information about a patient's health and treatment is disclosed only to those persons who need to be aware of that information in order to treat the patient effectively or minimise any risk of the patient harming himself or another person, or for the purposes of the proper administration of the establishment or agency.

(4) The registered person shall review the operation of each policy and procedure implemented under—

(a) this regulation;

(b) regulation 23; and

(c) in so far as they apply to him, regulations 35, 41(10), 45 and 46,

at intervals of not more than three years and shall, where appropriate, prepare and implement revised policies and procedures.

(5) The registered person shall make a copy of all written statements prepared in accordance with this regulation available for inspection by the Commission.

PART II

REGISTERED PERSONS

Fitness of registered provider

10.—(1) A person shall not carry on an establishment or agency unless he is fit to do so.

(2) A person is not fit to carry on an establishment or agency unless the person—

(a) is an individual, who carries on the establishment or agency—

(i) otherwise than in partnership with others, and he satisfies the requirements set out in paragraph (3);

(ii) in partnership with others, and he and each of his partners satisfies the requirements set out in paragraph (3);

(b) is a partnership, and each of the partners satisfies the requirements set out in paragraph (3);

(c) is an organisation and—

(i) the organisation has given notice to the Commission of the name, address and position in the organisation of an individual (in these Regulations referred to as "the responsible individual") who is a director, manager, secretary or other officer of the organisation and is responsible for supervising the management of the establishment or agency; and

(ii) that individual satisfies the requirements set out in paragraph (3).

[8]

(3) The requirements are that—

(a) he is of integrity and good character;

(b) he is physically and mentally fit to carry on the establishment or agency; and

(c) full and satisfactory information is available in relation to him—

(i) except where paragraph (4) applies, in respect of each of the matters specified in paragraphs 1 to 7 of Schedule 2;

(ii) where paragraph (4) applies, in respect of each of the matters specified in paragraphs 1 and 3 to 8 of Schedule 2.

(4) This paragraph applies where any certificate or information on any matters referred to in paragraph 2 of Schedule 2 is not available to an individual because any provision of the Police Act 1997(a) has not been brought into force.

(5) A person shall not carry on an establishment or agency if—

(a) he has been adjudged bankrupt or sequestration of his estate has been awarded and (in either case) he has not been discharged and the bankruptcy order has not been annulled or rescinded; or

(b) he has made a composition or arrangement with his creditors and has not been discharged in respect of it.

Appointment of manager

11.—(1) The registered provider shall appoint an individual to manage an establishment or agency if—

(a) there is no registered manager in respect of the establishment or agency; and

(b) the registered provider—

(i) is an organisation or a partnership;

(ii) is not a fit person to manage an establishment or agency; or

(iii) is not, or does not intend to be, in full-time day to day charge of the establishment or agency.

(2) Where the registered provider appoints a person to manage the establishment or agency, he shall forthwith give notice to the Commission of—

(a) the name of the person so appointed; and

(b) the date on which the appointment is to take effect.

Fitness of registered manager

12.—(1) A person shall not manage an establishment or agency unless he is fit to do so.

(2) A person is not fit to manage an establishment or agency unless—

(a) he is of integrity and good character;

(b) having regard to the size of the establishment or agency and the number and needs of the patients—

(i) he has the qualifications, skills and experience necessary to manage the establishment or agency; and

(ii) he is physically and mentally fit to do so; and

(c) full and satisfactory information is available in relation to him—

(i) except where paragraph (3) applies, in respect of each of the matters specified in paragraphs 1 to 7 of Schedule 2;

(ii) where paragraph (3) applies, in respect of each of the matters specified in paragraphs 1 and 3 to 8 of Schedule 2.

(3) This paragraph applies where any certificate or information on any matters referred to in paragraph 2 of Schedule 2 is not available to an individual because any provision of the Police Act 1997(b) has not been brought into force.

(a) 1997 c. 50. Sections 113 and 115, as amended, have not yet been brought into force. *See* the footnotes to paragraph 2 of Schedule 2.
(b) *See* footnote to regulation 10(4).

[9]

Registered person—general requirements

13.—(1) The registered provider and the registered manager shall, having regard to the size of the establishment or agency and the number and needs of the patients, carry on or (as the case may be) manage the establishment or agency with sufficient care, competence and skill.

(2) If the registered provider is—

(a) an individual, he shall undertake;

(b) an organisation, it shall ensure that the responsible individual undertakes;

(c) a partnership, it shall ensure that one of the partners undertakes,

from time to time such training as is appropriate to ensure that he has the skills necessary for carrying on the establishment or agency.

(3) The registered manager shall undertake from time to time such training as is appropriate to ensure that he has the skills necessary for managing the establishment or agency.

Notification of offences

14. Where the registered person or the responsible individual is convicted of any criminal offence, whether in England and Wales or elsewhere, he shall forthwith give notice in writing to the Commission of—

(a) the date and place of the conviction;

(b) the offence of which he was convicted; and

(c) the penalty imposed on him in respect of the offence.

PART III

CONDUCT OF HEALTH CARE ESTABLISHMENTS AND AGENCIES

CHAPTER 1

QUALITY OF SERVICE PROVISION

Quality of treatment and other service provision

15.—(1) Subject to regulation 6(3), the registered person shall provide treatment and any other services to patients in accordance with the statement of purpose, and shall ensure that the treatment and any other services provided to each patient—

(a) meet his individual needs;

(b) reflect published research evidence and guidance issued by the appropriate professional and expert bodies, as to good practice in the treatment of the condition from which the patient is suffering; and

(c) are (where necessary) provided by means of appropriate equipment.

(2) The registered person shall ensure that all equipment used in or for the purposes of the establishment, or for the purposes of the agency is—

(a) suitable for the purposes for which it is to be used; and

(b) properly maintained and in good working order.

(3) Where reusable medical devices are used in an establishment or agency, the registered person shall ensure that appropriate procedures are implemented in relation to cleaning, disinfection, inspection, packaging, sterilisation, transportation and storage of such devices.

(4) The procedures implemented in accordance with paragraph (3) shall be such as to ensure that reusable medical devices are handled safely and decontaminated effectively prior to re-use.

(5) The registered person shall make suitable arrangements for the ordering, recording, handling, safe keeping, safe administration and disposal of medicines used in or for the purposes of the establishment, or for the purposes of the agency.

(6) The registered person shall make suitable arrangements to minimise the risk of infection and toxic conditions and the spread of infection between patients and staff (including medical practitioners with practising privileges).

[10]

(7) If an establishment provides food for patients, the registered provider shall ensure that it is—

(a) provided in adequate quantities and at appropriate intervals;

(b) properly prepared, wholesome and nutritious; and

(c) suitable for the needs of patients,

and that the menu is varied at suitable intervals.

Care and welfare of patients

16.—(1) The registered person shall, so far as practicable, enable each patient to make decisions about matters affecting the way in which he is cared for and his general welfare.

(2) The registered person shall ensure that patients are permitted to control their own money, except where a patient does not wish, or lacks the capacity, to do so, in which case the registered person shall ensure that patient monies are properly held and recorded and that receipts are issued as appropriate.

(3) The registered person shall, so far as practicable, ascertain and take into account the wishes and feelings of all patients in determining the manner in which they are cared for and services are provided to them.

(4) The registered person shall make suitable arrangements to ensure that the establishment or agency is conducted—

(a) in a manner which respects the privacy and dignity of patients; and

(b) with due regard to the sex, religious and spiritual needs, racial origin, and cultural and linguistic background and any disability of patients.

(5) The registered provider and the registered manager (if any) shall each take all reasonable steps to ensure that the establishment or agency is conducted on the basis of good personal and professional relationships—

(a) between each other; and

(b) between each of them and the patients and staff.

Review of quality of treatment and other services

17.—(1) The registered person shall introduce and maintain a system for reviewing at appropriate intervals the quality of treatment and other services provided in or for the purposes of an establishment or for the purposes of an agency.

(2) The registered person shall supply to the Commission a report in respect of any review conducted by him for the purposes of paragraph (1) and make a copy of the report available to patients.

(3) The system referred to in paragraph (1) shall provide for consultation with patients and their representatives.

Staffing

18.—(1) The registered person shall, having regard to the nature of the establishment or agency and the number and needs of patients, ensure that there is at all times an appropriate number of suitably qualified, skilled and experienced persons employed in or for the purposes of the establishment or, as the case may be, for the purposes of the agency.

(2) The registered person shall ensure that each person employed in or for the purposes of the establishment or, for the purposes of the agency—

(a) receives appropriate training, supervision and appraisal;

(b) is enabled from time to time to obtain further qualifications appropriate to the work he performs; and

(c) is provided with a job description outlining his responsibilities.

(3) The registered person shall ensure that each person employed in or for the purposes of the establishment, or for the purposes of the agency and any medical practitioner with practising privileges, receives regular and appropriate appraisal and shall take such steps as may be necessary to address any aspect of—

(a) a health care professional's clinical practice; or

[11]

(b) the performance of a member of staff who is not a health care professional,

which is found to be unsatisfactory.

(4) The registered person shall take reasonable steps to ensure that any person working in an establishment or agency who is not employed by him and to whom paragraph (2) does not apply, is appropriately supervised while carrying out his duties.

Fitness of workers

19.—(1) The registered person shall ensure that—

(a) no person is employed to work in or for the purposes of the establishment or for the purposes of the agency; and

(b) no medical practitioner is granted consulting or practising privileges,

unless that person is fit to work in or for the purposes of the establishment, or for the purposes of the agency.

(2) A person is not fit to work in or for the purposes of an establishment, or for the purposes of an agency unless—

(a) he is of integrity and good character;

(b) he has the qualifications, skills and experience which are necessary for the work which he is to perform;

(c) he is physically and mentally fit for that work; and

(d) full and satisfactory information is available in relation to him—

(i) except where paragraph (3) applies, in respect to each of the matters specified in paragraphs 1 to 7 of Schedule 2;

(ii) where paragraph (3) applies, in respect of each of the matters specified in paragraphs 1 and 3 to 8 of Schedule 2.

(3) This paragraph applies where any certificate or information on any matters referred to in paragraph 2 of Schedule 2 is not available to an individual because any provision of the Police Act 1997(**a**) has not been brought into force.

Guidance for health care professionals

20. The registered person shall ensure that any code of ethics or professional practice prepared by a body which is responsible for regulation of members of a health care profession is made available in the establishment or agency to members of the health care profession in question.

Records

21.—(1) The registered person shall ensure that except in cases to which regulation 40(5) applies—

(a) a comprehensive medical record is maintained in relation to each patient, which includes—

(i) a contemporaneous note of all treatment provided to him;

(ii) his medical history and all other notes prepared by a health care professional about his case; and

(b) the record is retained for a period which is not less than that specified in Part I of Schedule 3 in relation to the type of patient in question or, where more than one such period could apply, the longest of them.

(2) The registered person shall ensure that—

(a) the medical record for a person who is currently a patient is kept in a secure place in the establishment or the agency premises; and

(b) the medical record for a person who is not currently a patient is stored securely (whether in the establishment or the agency premises or elsewhere) and that it can be located if required.

(**a**) *See* footnote to regulation 10(4).

(3) The registered person shall ensure that the records specified in Part II of Schedule 3 are maintained and that they are—

(a) kept up to date;

(b) at all times available for inspection in the establishment or the agency premises by any person authorised by the Commission to enter and inspect the establishment or agency premises; and

(c) retained for a period of not less than three years beginning on the date of the last entry.

Staff views as to conduct of establishment or agency

22.—(1) This regulation applies to any matter relating to the conduct of the establishment or agency so far as it may affect the health and welfare of patients.

(2) The registered person shall make arrangements to enable any person employed in or for the purposes of the establishment, or for the purposes of the agency, and any medical practitioner with practising privileges to inform the registered person and the Commission of their views about any matter to which this regulation applies.

Complaints

23.—(1) The registered person shall establish a procedure (in these Regulations referred to as "the complaints procedure") for considering complaints made to the registered person by a patient or a person acting on behalf of a patient.

(2) The registered person shall ensure that any complaint made under the complaints procedure is fully investigated.

(3) The registered person shall supply a written copy of the complaints procedure to every patient and, upon request, to—

(a) any person acting on behalf of a patient; and

(b) any person who is considering whether to become a patient.

(4) The written copy of the complaints procedure shall include—

(a) the name, address and telephone number of the Commission; and

(b) the procedure (if any) which has been notified by the Commission to the registered person for making complaints to the Commission relating to the establishment or agency.

(5) The registered person shall maintain a record of each complaint, including details of the investigations made, the outcome and any action taken in consequence and the requirements of regulation 21(3)(b) and (c) shall apply to that record.

(6) The registered person shall supply to the Commission annually a statement containing a summary of the complaints made during the preceding twelve months and the action taken in response.

Research

24.—(1) The registered person shall ensure that—

(a) before any research involving patients, information about patients, or bodily material and organs is undertaken in or for the purposes of an establishment, or for the purposes of an agency, a research proposal is prepared and approval is obtained from the appropriate Research Ethics Committee; and

(b) all such research projects include adequate safeguards for patients and employees.

(2) For the purposes of paragraph (1)(a), "the appropriate Research Ethics Committee" means a research ethics committee established in accordance with guidance issued from time to time by the Department of Health.

[13]

CHAPTER 2

PREMISES

Fitness of premises

25.—(1) Subject to regulation 6(3), the premises used as an establishment or agency must be in a location, and of a physical design and layout, which are suitable for the purpose of achieving the aims and objectives set out in the statement of purpose.

(2) The registered person shall ensure that—

(a) the premises are of sound construction and kept in a good state of repair externally and internally;

(b) the size and layout of rooms are suitable for the purposes for which they are to be used and are suitably equipped and furnished;

(c) all parts of the establishment or agency are kept clean and meet appropriate standards of hygiene;

(d) all parts of the establishment or agency to which patients have access are so far as reasonably practicable free from hazards to their safety; and

(e) if surgical procedures are undertaken, life support systems are used, or obstetric services and, in connection with childbirth, medical services, are provided in the establishment or agency, such electrical supply is provided during the interruption of public supply as is needed to safeguard the lives of the patients.

(3) The registered person shall provide for employees and medical practitioners with practising privileges—

(a) suitable facilities and accommodation, other than sleeping accommodation, including—

(i) facilities for the purpose of changing; and

(ii) storage facilities; and

(b) where the provision of such accommodation is needed by employees in connection with their work, sleeping accommodation.

(4) The registered person shall, after consultation with the fire authority—

(a) take adequate precautions against the risk of fire, including the provision and maintenance of suitable fire equipment;

(b) provide adequate means of escape in the event of a fire;

(c) make arrangements for persons employed in the establishment or for the purposes of the agency and medical practitioners to whom practising privileges have been granted to receive suitable training in fire prevention;

(d) ensure, by means of fire drills and practices at suitable intervals, that the persons employed in the establishment or for the purposes of the agency and, so far as practicable, patients and medical practitioners to whom practising privileges have been granted, are aware of the procedure to be followed in case of fire; and

(e) review fire precautions, the suitability of fire equipment and the procedure to be followed in case of fire at intervals not exceeding twelve months.

(5) In this regulation "fire authority", in relation to an establishment or agency, means the authority discharging in the area in which the establishment or agency is situated, the function of fire authority under the Fire Services Act 1947(**a**).

CHAPTER 3

MANAGEMENT

Visits by registered provider

26.—(1) Where the registered provider is an individual, but is not in day to day charge of the establishment or agency, he shall visit the establishment or agency premises in accordance with this regulation.

(**a**) 10 & 11 Geo. 6 c. 41.

[14]

(2) Where the registered provider is an organisation or a partnership, the establishment or agency shall be visited in accordance with this regulation by—

    (a) the responsible individual or one of the partners, as the case may be;

    (b) another of the directors or other persons responsible for the management of the organisation or partnership; or

    (c) an employee of the organisation or partnership who is not directly concerned with the conduct of the establishment or agency.

(3) Visits under paragraph (1) or (2) shall take place at least once every six months and shall be unannounced.

(4) The person carrying out the visit shall—

    (a) interview, with their consent and in private (if necessary, by telephone), such of the patients and their representatives and such employees as appears to him to be necessary in order to form an opinion of the standard of treatment and other services provided in or for the purposes of the establishment, or for the purposes of the agency;

    (b) inspect records of any complaints and, in the case of an establishment, its premises; and

    (c) prepare a written report on the conduct of the establishment or agency.

(5) The registered provider shall supply a copy of the report required to be made under paragraph (4)(c) to—

    (a) the Commission;

    (b) the registered manager; and

    (c) in the case of a visit under paragraph (2)—

        (i) where the registered provider is an organisation, to each of the directors or other persons responsible for the management of the organisation; and

        (ii) where the registered provider is a partnership, to each of the partners.

Financial position

27.—(1) The registered provider shall carry on the establishment or agency in such manner as is likely to ensure that the establishment or agency will be financially viable for the purpose of achieving the aims and objectives set out in the statement of purpose.

(2) The registered person shall, if the Commission so requests, provide the Commission with such information and documents as it may require for the purpose of considering the financial viability of the establishment or agency, including—

    (a) the annual accounts of the establishment or agency, certified by an accountant; or

    (b) the annual accounts of the organisation which is the registered provider of the establishment or agency, certified by an accountant, together with accounts relating to the establishment or agency itself.

(3) The registered person shall also provide the Commission with such other information as it may require in order to consider the financial viability of the establishment or agency, including—

    (a) a reference from a bank expressing an opinion as to the registered provider's financial standing;

    (b) information as to the financing and financial resources of the establishment or agency;

    (c) where the registered provider is a company, information as to any of its associated companies; and

    (d) a certificate of insurance for the registered provider in respect of liability which may be incurred by him in relation to the establishment or agency in respect of death, injury, public liability, damage or other loss.

(4) In this regulation, one company is associated with another if one of them has control of the other, or both are under the control of the same person.

[15]

CHAPTER 4

NOTICES TO BE GIVEN TO THE COMMISSION

Notification of events

28.—(1) The registered person shall give notice to the Commission of—

    (a) the death of a patient—

        (i) in an establishment;

        (ii) during treatment provided by an establishment or agency; or

        (iii) as a consequence of treatment provided by an establishment or agency within the period of seven days ending on the date of the death, and the circumstances of his death;

    (b) any serious injury to a patient;

    (c) the outbreak in an establishment of any infectious disease, which in the opinion of any medical practitioner employed in the establishment is sufficiently serious to be so notified;

    (d) any allegation of misconduct resulting in actual or potential harm to a patient by the registered person, any person employed in or for the purposes of the establishment or for the purposes of the agency, or any medical practitioner with practising privileges.

(2) Notice under paragraph (1) shall be given within the period of 24 hours beginning with the event in question and, if given orally, shall be confirmed in writing as soon as practicable.

Notice of absence

29.—(1) Where—

    (a) the registered provider, if he is the person in day to day charge of the establishment or agency; or

    (b) the registered manager,

proposes to be absent from the establishment or agency for a continuous period of 28 days or more, the registered person shall give notice in writing to the Commission of the proposed absence.

(2) Except in the case of an emergency, the notice referred to in paragraph (1) shall be given no later than one month before the proposed absence commences or within such shorter period as may be agreed with the Commission and the notice shall specify with respect to the proposed absence—

    (a) its length or expected length;

    (b) the reason for it;

    (c) the arrangements which have been made for running the establishment or agency;

    (d) the name, address and qualifications of the person who will be responsible for the establishment or agency during that absence; and

    (e) in the case of the absence of the registered manager, the arrangements that have been, or are proposed to be, made for appointing another person to manage the establishment or agency during that absence, including the proposed date by which the appointment is to be made.

(3) Where the absence arises as a result of an emergency, the registered person shall give notice of the absence within one week of its occurrence specifying the matters set out in sub-paragraphs (a) to (e) of paragraph (2).

(4) Where—

    (a) the registered provider, if he is the person in day to day charge of the establishment or agency; or

    (b) the registered manager,

has been absent from the establishment or agency for a continuous period of 28 days or more, and the Commission has not been given notice of the absence, the registered person shall, without delay, give notice in writing to the Commission of the absence, specifying the matters set out in paragraph (2)(a) to (e).

[16]

(5) The registered person shall notify the Commission of the return to duty of the registered provider or (as the case may be) the registered manager not later than 7 days after the date of his return.

Notice of changes

30. The registered person shall give notice in writing to the Commission as soon as it is practicable to do so if any of the following events take place or are proposed to take place—

    (a) a person other than the registered person carries on or manages the establishment or agency;

    (b) a person ceases to carry on or manage the establishment or agency;

    (c) where the registered person is an individual, he changes his name;

    (d) where the registered provider is a partnership, there is any change in the membership of the partnership;

    (e) where the registered provider is an organisation—

        (i) the name or address of the organisation is changed;

        (ii) there is any change of director, manager, secretary or other similar officer of the organisation;

        (iii) there is any change in the identity of the responsible individual;

    (f) where the registered provider is an individual, a trustee in bankruptcy is appointed;

    (g) where the registered provider is a company or partnership, a receiver, manager, liquidator or provisional liquidator is appointed; or

    (h) the premises of the establishment or agency are significantly altered or extended, or additional premises are acquired.

Appointment of liquidators etc.

31.—(1) Any person to whom paragraph (2) applies must—

    (a) forthwith notify the Commission of his appointment indicating the reasons for it;

    (b) appoint a manager to take full-time day to day charge of the establishment or agency in any case where there is no registered manager; and

    (c) before the end of the period of 28 days beginning on the date of his appointment, notify the Commission of his intentions regarding the future operation of the establishment or agency.

(2) This paragraph applies to any person appointed as—

    (a) the receiver or manager of the property of a company or partnership which is a registered provider of an establishment or agency;

    (b) liquidator or provisional liquidator of a company which is the registered provider of an establishment or agency;

    (c) the trustee in bankruptcy of a registered provider of an establishment or agency.

Death of registered person

32.—(1) If more than one person is registered in respect of an establishment or agency, and a registered person dies, the surviving registered person shall without delay notify the Commission of the death in writing.

(2) If only one person is registered in respect of an establishment or agency, and he dies, his personal representatives must notify the Commission in writing—

    (a) without delay of the death; and

    (b) within 28 days of their intentions regarding the future running of the establishment or agency.

(3) The personal representatives of the deceased registered provider may carry on the establishment or agency without being registered in respect of it—

    (a) for a period not exceeding 28 days; and

    (b) for any further period as may be determined in accordance with paragraph (4).

(4) The Commission may extend the period specified in paragraph (3)(a) by such further period, not exceeding one year, as the Commission shall determine, and shall notify any such determination to the personal representatives in writing.

[17]

(5) The personal representatives shall appoint a person to take full-time day to day charge of the establishment or agency during any period in which, in accordance with paragraph (3), they carry on the establishment or agency without being registered in respect of it.

PART IV

ADDITIONAL REQUIREMENTS APPLYING TO INDEPENDENT HOSPITALS

CHAPTER 1

PATHOLOGY SERVICES, RESUSCITATION AND TREATMENT OF CHILDREN IN INDEPENDENT HOSPITALS

Application of regulations 34 to 36

33.—(1) Regulations 34 to 36 apply to independent hospitals of the following kinds—

(a) those defined in section 2(3)(a)(i) of the Act except establishments excepted by regulation 3(2); and

(b) those in which medical treatment, including cosmetic surgery, is provided under anaesthesia or sedation.

(2) Regulation 34 also applies to any establishment or agency which provides pathology services.

Pathology services

34. The registered person shall ensure that—

(a) an adequate range of pathology services is available to meet the needs of the independent hospital;

(b) those services are provided to an appropriate standard;

(c) appropriate arrangements are made for the collection, and (where pathology services are provided outside the hospital) transportation of pathology specimens; and

(d) the patient from whom a specimen was taken, and such specimen, is identifiable at all times.

Resuscitation

35.—(1) The registered person shall prepare and implement a written statement of the policies to be applied and the procedures to be followed in the hospital in relation to resuscitation of patients, and shall review such statement annually.

(2) The registered person shall ensure that the policies and procedures implemented in accordance with paragraph (1)—

(a) take proper account of the right of all patients who are competent to do so to give or withhold consent to treatment;

(b) are available on request to every patient and any person acting on behalf of a patient; and

(c) are communicated to and understood by all employees and all medical practitioners with practising privileges who may be involved in decisions about resuscitation of a patient.

Treatment of children

36. The registered person shall ensure that, where a child is treated in an independent hospital—

(a) he is treated in accommodation which is separate from accommodation in which adult patients are treated;

(b) particular medical, physical, psychological, social, educational and supervision needs arising from his age are met;

[18]

(c) his treatment is provided by persons who have appropriate qualifications, skills and experience in the treatment of children;

(d) his parents are kept fully informed of his condition and so far as is practicable consulted about all aspects of his treatment, except where the child is himself competent to consent to treatment and does not wish his parents to be so informed and consulted.

CHAPTER 2

INDEPENDENT HOSPITALS IN WHICH CERTAIN LISTED SERVICES ARE PROVIDED

Surgical procedures

37.—(1) Where medical treatment (including cosmetic surgery) is provided under anaesthesia or sedation in an independent hospital, the registered person shall ensure that—

(a) each operating theatre is designed, equipped and maintained to an appropriate standard for the purposes for which it is to be used;

(b) all surgery is carried out by, or under the direction of, a suitably qualified, skilled and experienced medical practitioner;

(c) an appropriate number of suitably qualified, skilled and experienced employees are in attendance during each surgical procedure; and

(d) the patient receives appropriate treatment—

(i) before administration of an anaesthetic or sedation;

(ii) whilst undergoing a surgical procedure;

(iii) during recovery from general anaesthesia; and

(iv) post-operatively.

(2) The registered person shall ensure that before a patient consents to any surgery offered by the independent hospital, he has received clear and comprehensive information about the procedure and any risks associated with it.

(3) In the case of a patient who is not competent to consent to surgery, the information mentioned in paragraph (2) shall, wherever possible, be provided to his representatives.

Dental treatment under general anaesthesia

38. Where the treatment provided in an independent hospital includes dental treatment under general anaesthesia, the registered person shall ensure that—

(a) the dentist and any employees assisting him are suitably qualified, skilled and experienced to deal with any emergency which occurs during or as a result of the general anaesthesia or treatment; and

(b) adequate facilities, drugs and equipment are available to deal with any such emergency.

Obstetric services—staffing

39.—(1) This regulation and regulation 40 apply to an independent hospital in which obstetric services and, in connection with childbirth, medical services are provided.

(2) The registered person shall appoint a Head of Midwifery Services who is responsible for managing the provision of midwifery services in an independent hospital and, except in cases where obstetric services are provided in the hospital primarily by midwives, a Head of Obstetric Services whose name is included in the specialist medical register in respect of a specialty in obstetrics and who is responsible for managing the provision of obstetric services.

(3) The registered person shall ensure that the health care professional who is primarily responsible for caring for pregnant women and assisting at childbirth is a midwife, an appropriately qualified general practitioner, or a medical practitioner whose name is included in the specialist medical register in respect of a specialty in obstetrics.

(4) Where obstetric services are provided in an independent hospital primarily by midwives, the registered person shall ensure that the services of a medical practitioner who is competent to deal with obstetric emergencies are available at all times.

[19]

(5) The registered person shall ensure that a health care professional who is competent to undertake resuscitation of a new born baby is available in the hospital at all times and that his skills are regularly reviewed and, if necessary, updated.

Obstetric services—further requirements

40.—(1) The registered person shall ensure that—

(a) any death of a patient in an independent hospital during, or as a result of, pregnancy or childbirth; and

(b) any still-birth or neonatal death in an independent hospital,

are reported to any person undertaking an enquiry into such deaths on behalf of the Secretary of State(**a**).

(2) The registered person shall ensure that facilities are available within the hospital to provide adequate treatment to patients who have undergone a delivery requiring surgical intervention or the use of forceps and that such patients are cared for by an appropriately experienced midwife.

(3) The registered person shall ensure that appropriate arrangements are in place for the immediate transfer, where necessary, of a patient and her new born child to critical care facilities within the hospital or elsewhere in the near vicinity.

(4) The registered person shall ensure that appropriate arrangements are in place for the treatment and, if necessary transfer to a specialist care facility, of a very sick patient or new born child.

(5) The registered person shall ensure that a maternity record is maintained for each patient receiving obstetric services and each child born in the hospital, which—

(a) includes the details specified in regulation 21(1)(a) and in Parts I and II of Schedule 4; and

(b) is retained for a period of not less than 25 years beginning on the date of the last entry,

and the requirements of regulation 21(2) shall apply to that record.

(6) In this regulation—

"still-birth" has the meaning given to it in the Births and Deaths Registration Act 1953(**b**);

"neonatal death" means the death of a child before the end of the period of 28 days beginning with the date of the child's birth.

Termination of pregnancies

41.—(1) This regulation applies to an independent hospital in which termination of pregnancies takes place.

(2) The registered person shall ensure that no patient is admitted to the hospital for termination of a pregnancy, and that no fee is demanded or accepted from a patient in respect of a termination, unless two certificates of opinion have been received in respect of the patient.

(3) The registered person shall ensure that a certificate of opinion in respect of a patient undergoing termination of a pregnancy is completed and included with the patient's record, within the meaning of regulation 21.

(4) The registered person shall ensure that no termination of a pregnancy is undertaken after the 20th week of gestation, unless—

(a) the patient is treated by persons who are suitably qualified, skilled and experienced in the late termination of pregnancy; and

(b) appropriate procedures are in place to deal with any medical emergency which occurs during or as a result of the termination.

(5) The registered person shall ensure that no termination of a pregnancy is undertaken after the 24th week of gestation.

(**a**) The Confidential Enquiry into Maternal Deaths and the Confidential Enquiry into Stillbirths and Deaths in Infancy are currently undertaken on behalf of the Secretary of State for Health by the National Institute for Clinical Excellence.
(**b**) 1953 c. 20. *See* section 41, as amended by the Still-Birth (Definition) Act 1992 (c. 29), section 1(1).

[20]

(6) The registered person shall ensure that a register of patients undergoing termination of a pregnancy in the hospital is maintained, which is—

(a) separate from the register of patients which is to be maintained under paragraph 1 of Schedule 3;

(b) completed in respect of each patient at the time the termination is undertaken; and

(c) retained for a period of not less than three years beginning on the date of the last entry.

(7) The registered person shall ensure that a record is maintained of the total numbers of terminations undertaken in the hospital; and the requirements of regulation 21(3) shall apply to that record.

(8) The registered person shall ensure that notice in writing is sent to the Chief Medical Officer of the Department of Health of each termination of pregnancy which takes place in the hospital(**a**).

(9) If the registered person—

(a) receives information concerning the death of a patient who has undergone termination of a pregnancy in the hospital during the period of 12 months ending on the date on which the information is received; and

(b) has reason to believe that the patient's death may be associated with the termination,

he shall give notice in writing to the Commission of that information, within the period of 14 days beginning on the day on which the information is received.

(10) The registered person shall prepare and implement appropriate procedures in the hospital to ensure that fetal tissue is treated with respect.

(11) In this regulation, "certificate of opinion" means a certificate required by regulations made under section 2(1) of the Abortion Act 1967(**b**).

Use of certain techniques or technology

42.—(1) The registered person shall ensure that no Class 3B or Class 4 laser or intense light source (within the meaning of regulation 3(1)), is used in or for the purposes of an independent hospital unless that hospital has in place a professional protocol drawn up by a trained and experienced medical practitioner or dentist from the relevant discipline in accordance with which treatment is to be provided, and is so provided.

(2) The registered person shall ensure that such a laser or intense light source is used in or for the purposes of the hospital only by a person who has undertaken appropriate training and has demonstrated an understanding of—

(a) the correct use of the equipment in question;

(b) the risks associated with using a laser or intense light source;

(c) its biological and environmental effects;

(d) precautions to be taken before and during use of a laser or intense light source; and

(e) action to be taken in the event of an accident, emergency, or other adverse incident.

CHAPTER 3

MENTAL HEALTH HOSPITALS

Application of regulations 44 to 47

43. Regulations 44 to 47 apply to independent hospitals of the following kinds—

(a) those, the main purpose of which, is to provide medical or psychiatric treatment for mental disorder; and

(b) those in which treatment or nursing (or both) are provided for persons liable to be detained under the Mental Health Act 1983(**c**).

(**a**) *See* S.I. 1991/499, which requires such notice to be given by the medical practitioner carrying out the termination.
(**b**) 1967 c. 87. *See* S.I. 1991/499.
(**c**) 1983 c. 20.

[21]

Safety of patients and others

44.—(1) The statement of policies and procedures which is to be prepared and implemented by the registered person in accordance with regulation 9(1)(e) shall include policies and procedures in relation to—

(a) assessment of a patient's propensity to violence and self harm;

(b) the provision of information to employees as to the outcome of such an assessment;

(c) assessment of the effect of the layout of the hospital premises, and its policies and procedures, on the risk of a patient harming himself or another person; and

(d) the provision of training to enable employees to minimise the risk of a patient harming himself or another person.

(2) The registered person shall in particular prepare and implement a suicide protocol in the hospital which requires—

(a) a comprehensive examination of the mental condition of each patient;

(b) an evaluation of the patient's history of mental disorder, including identification of suicidal tendencies;

(c) an assessment of the patient's propensity to suicide; and

(d) if necessary, appropriate action to reduce the risk of the patient committing suicide.

Management of disturbed behaviour

45. The registered person shall prepare and implement a written policy setting out—

(a) how disturbed behaviour exhibited by a patient is to be managed;

(b) permitted measures of restraint and the circumstances in which they may be used;

(c) requirements for employees to report serious incidents of violence or self harm, including guidance as to how those incidents should be classified; and

(d) the procedure for review of such incidents and determination of the action which is to be taken subsequently.

Visitors

46. The registered person shall prepare and implement written policies and procedures in the hospital in relation to patients receiving visitors.

Mental health records

47. The registered person shall ensure that any records which are required to be made under the Mental Health (Hospital, Guardianship and Consent to Treatment) Regulations 1983(**a**), and which relate to the detention or treatment of a patient in an independent hospital, are kept for a period of not less than five years beginning on the date on which the person to whom they relate ceases to be a patient in the hospital.

PART V

ADDITIONAL REQUIREMENTS APPLYING TO INDEPENDENT CLINICS

Independent clinics

48. Where an independent clinic provides antenatal care to patients, the registered person shall ensure that the health care professional who is primarily responsible for providing that care is a midwife, an appropriately qualified general practitioner, or a medical practitioner with a specialist qualification in obstetrics.

(**a**) S.I. 1983/893, as amended.

[22]

PART VI

ADDITIONAL REQUIREMENTS APPLYING TO INDEPENDENT MEDICAL AGENCIES

Independent medical agencies

49. The registered person shall ensure that the register of patients to be maintained in relation to an independent medical agency under paragraph 1 of Schedule 3 includes the name of the medical practitioner by whom each patient is treated.

PART VII

MISCELLANEOUS

Compliance with regulations

50. Where there is more than one registered person in respect of an establishment or agency, anything which is required under these Regulations to be done by the registered person shall, if done by one of the registered persons, not be required to be done by any of the other registered persons.

Offences

51.—(1) A contravention, or failure to comply with, any of the provisions of regulations 6, 7, 9, 14, 15, 16(1) to (4), 17 to 32, 34 to 42 and 44 to 49 shall be an offence.

(2) The Commission shall not bring proceedings against a person in respect of any contravention or failure to comply with those regulations unless—

    (a) subject to paragraph (4), he is a registered person;

    (b) notice has been given to him in accordance with paragraph (3);

    (c) the period specified in the notice, beginning with the date of the notice has expired; and

    (d) the person contravenes or fails to comply with any of the provisions of the regulations mentioned in the notice.

(3) Where the Commission considers that the registered person has contravened or failed to comply with any of the provisions of the regulations mentioned in paragraph (1), it may serve a notice on the registered person specifying—

    (a) in what respect in its opinion the registered person has contravened or is contravening any of the regulations, or has failed or is failing to comply with the requirements of any of the regulations;

    (b) what action, in the opinion of the Commission, the registered person should take so as to comply with any of those regulations; and

    (c) the period, not exceeding three months beginning on the date on which the notice is given, within which the registered person should take action.

(4) The Commission may bring proceedings against a person who was once, but no longer is a registered person, in respect of a failure to comply with regulation 21 and for this purpose, references in paragraphs (2) and (3) to a registered person shall be taken to include such a person.

Signed by authority of the Secretary of State for Health

Jacqui Smith
Minister of State,
Department of Health

11th December 2001

[23]

SCHEDULE 1 Regulation 6

INFORMATION TO BE INCLUDED IN THE STATEMENT OF PURPOSE

1. The aims and objectives of the establishment or agency.

2. The name and address of the registered provider and of any registered manager.

3. The relevant qualifications and experience of the registered provider and any registered manager.

4. The number, relevant qualifications and experience of the staff working in the establishment, or for the purposes of the agency.

5. The organisational structure of the establishment or agency.

6. The kinds of treatment and any other services provided for the purposes of the establishment or agency, the range of needs which those services are intended to meet and the facilities which are available for the benefit of patients.

7. The arrangements made for consultation with patients about the operation of the establishment or agency.

8. The arrangements made for contact between any in-patients and their relatives, friends and representatives.

9. The arrangements for dealing with complaints.

10. The arrangements for respecting the privacy and dignity of patients.

SCHEDULE 2 Regulations 10(3), 12(2) and 19(2)

INFORMATION REQUIRED IN RESPECT OF PERSONS SEEKING TO CARRY ON, MANAGE OR WORK AT AN ESTABLISHMENT OR AGENCY

1. Positive proof of identity including a recent photograph.

2. Either—

(a) where the certificate is required for a purpose relating to section 115(5)(ea) of the Police Act 1997 (registration under Part II of the Care Standards Act 2000)(**a**), or the position falls within section 115(3) or (4) of that Act(**b**), an enhanced criminal record certificate issued under section 115 of that Act; or

(b) in any other case, a criminal record certificate issued under section 113 of that Act,

including, where applicable, the matters specified in section 113(3A) or (3C) or 115(6A) or (6B) of that Act(**c**).

3. Two written references, being references from the person's most recent employers, if any.

4. Where a person has previously worked in a position which involved work with children or vulnerable adults, verification, so far as reasonably practicable, of the reason why he ceased to work in that position.

5. Documentary evidence of any relevant qualifications.

6. A full employment history, together with a satisfactory written explanation of any gaps in employment.

7. Where he is a health care professional, details of his registration with the body (if any) responsible for regulation of members of the health care profession in question.

8. Details of any criminal offences—

(a) of which the person has been convicted, including details of any convictions which are spent within the meaning of section 1 of the Rehabilitation of Offenders Act 1974(**d**) and which may be disclosed by virtue of the Rehabilitation of Offenders (Exceptions) Order 1975(**e**); or

---

(**a**) Section 115(5)(ea) is inserted by the Care Standards Act 2000, section 104, on a date to be appointed. Sections 113 and 115, as amended, have not yet been brought into force.

(**b**) A position is within section 115(3) if it involves regularly caring for, training, supervising or being in sole charge of persons aged under 18. A position is within section 115(4) if it is of a kind specified in regulations and involves regularly caring for, training, supervising or being in sole charge of persons aged 18 or over.

(**c**) Sections 113(3A) and 115(6A) are added to the Police Act 1997 by section 8 of the Protection of Children Act 1999 c. 14 on a date to be appointed, and amended by section 104 and 116 of, and paragraph 25 of Schedule 4 to, the Care Standards Act 2000. Sections 113(3C) and 115(6B) are added to the Police Act 1997 by section 90 of the Care Standards Act 2000 on a date to be appointed.

(**d**) 1974 c. 53.

(**e**) S.I. 1975/1023. Relevant amendments have been made by S.I. 1986/1249, S.I. 1986/2268 and S.I. 2001/1192.

[24]

(b) in respect of which he has been cautioned by a constable and which, at the time the caution was given, he admitted.

SCHEDULE 3   Regulation 21(1), (3)

PART I

PERIOD FOR WHICH MEDICAL RECORDS MUST BE RETAINED

Type of patient	Minimum period of retention
(a) Patient who was under the age of 17 at the date on which the treatment to which the records refer was concluded.	Until the patient's 25th birthday.
(b) Patient who was aged 17 at the date on which the treatment to which the records refer was concluded.	Until the patient's 26th birthday.
(c) Patient who died before attaining the age of 18.	A period of 8 years beginning on the date of the patient's death.
(d) Patient who was treated for mental disorder during the period to which the records refer.	A period of 20 years beginning on the date of the last entry in the record.
(e) Patient who was treated for mental disorder during the period to which the records refer and who died whilst receiving that treatment.	A period of 8 years beginning on the date of the patient's death.
(f) Patient whose records relate to treatment by a general practitioner.	A period of 10 years beginning on the date of the last entry.
(g) Patient who has received an organ transplant.	A period of 11 years beginning on the date of the patient's death or discharge whichever is the earlier.
(h) All other cases.	A period of 8 years beginning on the date of the last entry in the record.

PART II

RECORDS TO BE MAINTAINED FOR INSPECTION

1. A register of patients, including—
   (a) the name, address, telephone number, date of birth and marital status of each patient;
   (b) the name, address and telephone number of the patient's next of kin or any person authorised by the patient to act on his behalf;
   (c) the name, address and telephone number of the patient's general practitioner;
   (d) where the patient is a child, the name and address of the school which he attends or attended before admission to an establishment;
   (e) where a patient has been received into guardianship under the Mental Health Act 1983, the name, address and telephone number of the guardian;
   (f) the name and address of any body which arranged the patient's admission or treatment;
   (g) the date on which the patient was admitted to an establishment or first received treatment provided for the purposes of an establishment or agency;
   (h) the nature of the treatment for which the patient was admitted or which he received;
   (i) where the patient has been an in-patient in an independent hospital, the date of his discharge;
   (j) if the patient has been transferred to a hospital (including a health service hospital), the date of the transfer, the reasons for it and the name of the hospital to which the patient was transferred;
   (k) if the patient dies whilst in an establishment or during treatment provided for the purposes of an establishment or agency, the date, time and cause of his death.

2. A register of all surgical operations performed in an establishment or by an agency, including—
   (a) the name of the patient on whom the operation was performed;
   (b) the nature of the surgical procedure and the date on which it took place;
   (c) the name of the medical practitioner or dentist by whom the operation was performed;
   (d) the name of the anaesthetist in attendance;

[25]

(e) the name and signature of the person responsible for checking that all needles, swabs and equipment used during the operation have been recovered from the patient;

(f) details of all implanted medical devices, except where this would entail the disclosure of information contrary to the provisions of section 33(5) of the Human Fertilisation and Embryology Act 1990 (restrictions on disclosure of information).

3. A register of each occasion on which a technique or technology to which regulation 42 applies has been used; including—

(a) the name of the patient in connection with whose treatment the technique or technology was used;

(b) the nature of the technique or technology in question and the date on which it was used; and

(c) the name of the person using it.

4. A register of all mechanical and technical equipment used for the purposes of treatment provided by the establishment or agency including—

(a) the date of purchase of the equipment;

(b) the date of installation of the equipment;

(c) details of maintenance of the equipment and the dates on which maintenance work was carried out.

5. A register of all events which must be notified to the Commission in accordance with regulation 28.

6. A record of the rostered shifts for each employee and a record of the hours actually worked by each person.

7. A record of each person employed in or for the purposes of the establishment, or for the purposes of the agency and each medical practitioner to whom practising privileges have been granted, including—

(a) his name and date of birth;

(b) details of his position in the establishment or agency;

(c) dates of employment; and

(d) in respect of a health care professional, details of his professional qualifications and registration with his professional regulatory body.

SCHEDULE 4   Regulation 40(5)(a)

PART I

DETAILS TO BE RECORDED IN RESPECT OF PATIENTS RECEIVING OBSTETRIC SERVICES

1. The date and time of delivery of each patient, the number of children born to the patient, the sex of each child and whether the birth was a live birth or a stillbirth.

2. The name and qualifications of the person who delivered the patient.

3. The date and time of any miscarriage occurring in the hospital.

4. The date on which any child born to a patient left the hospital.

5. If any child born to a patient died in the hospital, the date and time of death.

PART II

DETAILS TO BE RECORDED IN RESPECT OF A CHILD BORN IN AN INDEPENDENT HOSPITAL

1. Details of the weight and condition of the child at birth.

2. A daily statement of the child's health.

3. If any paediatric examination is carried out involving any of the following procedures—

(a) examination for congenital abnormalities including congenital dislocation of the hip;

(b) measurement of the circumference of the head of the child;

(c) measurement of the length of the child;

(d) screening for phenylketonuria,

details of such examination and the result.

[26]

EXPLANATORY NOTE

(This note is not part of the Regulations)

These Regulations are made under the Care Standards Act 2000 ("the Act"), and apply to England only. Part I of the Act establishes, in relation to England, the National Care Standards Commission ("the Commission") and Part II provides for the registration and inspection of establishments and agencies, including private and voluntary health care establishments and agencies, by the Commission. It also provides powers for regulations governing the conduct of establishments and agencies. The majority of Parts I and II of the Act (in so far as not already in force) will be brought into force on 1 April 2002.

Regulation 3 provides that "listed services" include treatment using the prescribed techniques and technology set out in regulation 3(1). Regulation 3(2) then excepts certain techniques and technology from being listed services, and regulation 3(2) excludes certain establishments from the definition of an independent hospital under section 2 of the Act. These include establishments providing medical or psychiatric treatment but which have no overnight beds for patients, establishments which are service hospitals under the Armed Forces Act 1981, or which are establishments catering for offenders under the Prison Act 1952. In addition, independent clinics (as defined in these Regulations) are excluded, as are establishments where general practitioners provide NHS services, but where there may be a small minority of private patients who also receive treatment. The private residence of a patient is also excluded provided that treatment is provided there only to that patient, as are surgeries and consulting rooms (which are separate from a hospital) which provide medical services under arrangements made on behalf of patients by their employers or others, and sports grounds and gymnasia where treatment is given to those taking part in sporting activities and events.

Regulation 3(4) modifies the definition of cosmetic surgery for the purpose of section 2(7) of the Act.

Regulation 4 defines the meaning of the term "independent clinic" and regulation 5 excepts certain establishments from being an independent medical agency.

By regulation 6, each establishment or agency must have a statement of purpose consisting of the matters set out in Schedule 1, and a patients' guide to the establishment or agency. The establishment or agency must be carried on in a manner which is consistent with the statement of purpose.

Regulation 9 sets out the policies and procedures which must be prepared and implemented in relation to an establishment.

Regulations 10 to 14 make provision about the fitness of the persons carrying on and managing an establishment or agency and require satisfactory information to be obtained in relation to the matters prescribed in Schedule 2. Where the provider is an organisation, it must nominate a responsible individual in respect of whom this information must be available (regulation 10). Regulation 11 prescribes the circumstances where a manager must be appointed for the establishment or agency, and regulation 13 imposes general requirements in relation to the proper conduct of the establishment or agency, and the need for appropriate training.

Part III makes provision about the conduct of establishments or agencies, in particular about the quality of the services to be provided in an establishment or agency, including matters relating to privacy, dignity and religious observance, the staffing of the establishment or agency and the fitness of workers and about complaints and record keeping (regulation 21 and Schedule 3). Provision is also made about the suitability of premises and the fire precautions to be taken and the management of establishments and agencies. The registered provider is required to visit the establishment or agency as prescribed (regulation 26), and regulation 27 imposes requirements relating to the financial viability of the establishment or agency. Regulations 28 to 32 deal with the giving of notices to the Commission.

[27]

Part IV and Schedule 4 set out additional requirements that apply to independent hospitals, and Parts V and VI set out additional requirements applying to independent clinics and independent medical agencies.

Part VII deals with miscellaneous matters. In particular, regulation 51 provides for offences. A breach of regulations 6, 7, 9, 14, 15, 16(1) to (4), 17 to 32, 34 to 42 and 44 to 49 may found an offence on the part of the registered person. However, no prosecution may be brought unless the Commission has given the registered person a notice which sets out in what respect it is alleged he is not complying with a regulation, and what action, and by when, the Commission considers is necessary in order to comply with the regulation.

Printed in the United Kingdom r.
ID. 162440, C10, 1/04 5673